LEGENDARY HORSEMEN

THE FORCE MARCH WEST

LEGENDARY HORSEMEN

IMAGES OF THE CANADIAN WEST

PAINTINGS BY ROBERT MAGEE

TEXT BY GORDON JAREMKO & DAVID FINCH

PUBLISHED BY THE OH RANCH
LONGVIEW, ALBERTA

This book is published on the occasion of the opening of The Western Heritage Centre at Cochrane, Alberta, 1996.
Most of the paintings in this book are exhibited at The Western Heritage Centre.

Compilation copyright © 1996 by The OH Ranch Ltd.

Paintings copyrights © 1996 by D.K. (Doc) Seaman, O.C., B.Sc., L.L.D., and Robert Magee

Text copyrights © 1996 by Gordon Jaremko, David Finch and Patrick Stiles

FIRST EDITION

CANADIAN CATALOGUING IN PUBLICATION DATA

Magee, Robert, 1932 –
Legendary horsemen: images of the Canadian West: paintings

ISBN 0-9680604-0-4

1. Magee, Robert, 1932 - 2. Canada, Western, in art. 3. Horsemen and horsewomen in art.
4. Canada, Western–History. I. Finch, David, 1956 – II. Jaremko, Gordon. III. OH Ranch. IV. Western Heritage Centre. V. Title.

ND249.M329A4 1996   759.11   C96-900191-6

Published by The OH Ranch
Box 52, Longview, Alberta, Canada
T0L 1H0

Printed in China by Book Art Inc., Markham, Ontario, Canada

CONTENTS

PREFACE

THE ARTIST AND WRITERS have my personal congratulations for their respective parts in bringing added distinction to the already rich legacy of famous horses and horsemanship. The artist used the horse in his paintings to contribute meaning and emotion to those seeking a more personal understanding of our Western Canadian heritage. The saga of the marvellous Native horsemen of the buffalo era, and the parade of significant events that were part of the frontier story all feature the horse as part of the tale. This book is a tribute to them all.

The first generation of farmers in Western Canada came with oxen, but invariably switched to horses when supply and price warranted. Similarly, many farmers kept their horses long after steam and tractor power became fashionable. To the cowboy, the horse remains a loyal working companion.

There was a time when every western farmer was a horseman . . . and a good one . . . and his sons aspired to be good horsemen like their fathers. Every rural district became an unorganized community of horsemen. The heavy horse classes became the best excuse for conducting a fair. A Saturday trip to town gave sufficient reason for polishing the heavy harness, rolling manes, and harnessing with top collars. Horsemen became proud citizens, and most of them cultivated feelings of sympathy for their horses on account of the heavy toil and privation to which they were often exposed. One of the MacEwan family neighbours in Melfort, Saskatchewan admitted that he expected to face his horses as Judges when he came to the Pearly Gates, and he hoped they'd be friendly.

Still, too many horses suffered and not enough experienced the realization of a dearly-bought retirement. I hesitate about using my father as one of the inspiring horsemen of my memory, but believe I must. Alexander MacEwan, when leaving the family farm in 1946 authorized the usual dispersal by auction of cattle, poultry, machinery, home furnishings, and supplies, but not his horses. The latter would remain on the farm that had become their only home, there to be assured of feed and merciful care until the natural ends of their lives. The arrangement was one the father made with the neighbour, anxious to buy the one section farm at $50 per acre. But by the new "deal," the purchaser, with a reputation for mercy towards horses, bought the section for exactly half the bartered price because he had agreed to honour MacEwan's wish that his greatly-loved horses would enjoy the luxury of a well-earned retirement in a place they had known since birth.

Horse training became a popular pastime and a moderately profitable profession. The common techniques ranged from gentle treatment to rougher and even cruel handling and precipitated the ongoing debate over the best way to break horses. It would probably be easy, even in 1995, to revive some of those old debates that were expected to declare in favour of the "slow and easy," or "fast and rough" method of horse training. If this old horseman of 1995 was confronted by the necessity of a decision from other years, he might escape with the minimum blemish by simply declaring what he had said before, that the most skilful horse handler from his years of observation is, without reservation, his friend and former breeder of Arabian horses, Chick Miller of Olds, Alberta.

To conclude, I draw from the inspired verses of Captain Stanley Harrison, farmer, conservationist, artist, poet, soldier and scholar. Early in World War One, Harrison joined for service in a cavalry unit and took his own horse to war with him. Man and horse were already old friends and one of his most bitter wartime experiences was in having his beloved equine companion shot from under him at Paschendale in 1917. Therein, Harrison confessed his belief in the immortality of the souls of great horses:

Somewhere . . . Somewhere in Time's own space,
There must be some sweet-pastured place.
Where creeks sing on and tall trees grow,
Some Paradise where horses go.
For by the love that guides my pen,
I know great horses live again.

Grant MacEwan
Calgary, September, 1995

GRANT MACEWAN

HORSEMAN TOMMY BEWS

Cowboys and their horses have long been inseparable. The horse is the cowboy's means of transport, his principal tool, his friend and his constant companion.

INTRODUCTION

Westerners like Al Red Crow, Francis Gardner and Paula Harris know why horsepower survived the conversion of pounds, miles and acres to kilograms, kilometres and hectares. Horsepower spells culture, work, recreation and community. Red Crow is a Plains Native, Gardner ranches in the Rocky Mountain foothills, and Harris is a newcomer to the West. And although the three have never met, a meeting of the minds does occur. It happens on horseback.

Red Crow belongs to a society which calls itself the Siksika (Blackfoot) Nation. When he rides past the landmark Castle Junction in Banff National Park, he does not see Castle Mountain. He sees Mii-Stux-Koo-Wa, or Big Rock. He sees an assembly ground and place of healing. It was ancient and sacred long before Francis Gardner's English grandfather ever dreamed of emigrating a century ago. Red Crow sees 27 square miles (70 km²) which Canada's Treaty Seven promised to his ancestors and their descendants in 1877, for as long as the rivers flow and the sun rises. In 1902, the federal government, without asking, declared the mountain citadel part of the national park.

To revive that memory and remind Canada of its original promise, Red Crow and his neighbours return every autumn to the site of the treaty signing at Blackfoot Crossing, about 60 miles (100 km) east of Calgary on the Bow River. There, they mount horses and embark on a Na-Soo-Wa, a cross between a warrior mission and a pilgrimage akin to the Medieval Crusades. Horses are a symbolic and vital part of this mission, partly because they traditionally represented power and prestige to Natives, and also because the ride brings the treaty signing back to life. Dismounting occasionally for drum chants to appease the Creator and to keep adrenaline flowing, the Siksika ride 185 miles (300 km) west along the Trans-Canada, passing through Calgary before reaching their destination at Castle Junction.

Francis Gardner has a mission too. And he, too, crusades on horseback. He mounts up every morning — rain, shine, subarctic blow or house-shaking Chinook gale — and heads out across his 14-square-mile (34 km²) heritage. Gardner's Mount Sentinel Ranch lies in the calendar-picture country of the foothills south of Longview. It's a 500-head operation which Gardner

THE BUFFALO RUNNER

A young Blackfoot warrior and two Barbs
(the favourite horse of the Blackfoot)
on their way to the hunt. The buffalo
runner is leading his principal hunting
horse out of respect for it as much as
to conserve its energy.

runs with just 16 horses. He needs to be economical. Even at peaks of beef market cycles, cattle prices fall far short of production costs for all but the biggest outfits.

Gardner needs to be just as careful with his hills as his money. And he needs no lectures from environmentalists. If he fails to conserve and protect his land, there will be no grass, no cattle and nothing on the table for him and his family. With blunt eloquence, he voices the consensus of a range fraternity which runs from 19th-century pioneer heirs like himself to D.K. (Doc) Seaman, who won the community's heart in 1987 by buying the historic OH Ranch and keeping it going as a cattle spread worked on horseback. (Seaman outmanoeuvred Canada's Department of National Defence, which wanted a practice range for cannons, tanks and heavily-equipped troops.)

Territorial expansion is becoming increasingly out of the question for ranchers, mainly because acreage hunters and tourism ventures from the city of Calgary, little more than an hour's drive to the north, are driving real estate prices up. "We're 100 percent cattle and 90 percent broke," Gardner says. "You can't justify paying money for land in the ranching business these days. You're in it for something else. It sure isn't for cash flow." What else? "I guess it's to be a part of the natural world." Working on horseback with range cattle comes as naturally as riding down buffalo did to the Natives. "You can't expect to integrate yourself with this country if you don't do it on horseback. Any kind of mechanization doesn't fit. The hills are too steep. The bogs are too soft. The bush is too thick. Machinery destroys the country. If you want to decimate an environment, you throw in horsepower with diesel engines."

In Calgary, Paula Harris has always felt a need to integrate with the environment and community that became her home by adoption. Not unlike many Natives and ranchers, she has found horses to be the answer to this need. Weekdays, Harris works in the mainstream of urban industrial society, teaching English to trades students at the Southern Alberta Institute of Technology. Evenings and weekends, she grooms and rides Phoenix Sun, a registered Quarter horse.

The desire to mount up was among Harris' earliest childhood yearnings in her southern Ontario home town of St. Catherine's. Whenever possible, she got her parents to take gravel back roads around the Toronto region, so she could admire horses through the windows of the family car. High points included trips past Windfield Farms, magnate E.P. Taylor's celebrated thoroughbred stable and home of Northern Dancer. But a horse of her own remained out of the question.

Harris' relocation in 1979 to the West's wide-open spaces finally created a chance for girlhood dreams to come true. Indeed, the West lived up to its reputation as the land of opportunity. Within six years, she bought a pony, and after a five-year apprenticeship,

13

LION OF THE FRONTIER

Sam Steele first came west as an up-and-coming young sergeant with the newly recruited force. Steele served with élan and distinction in several posts, rising to the rank of superintendent.

moved up to her Phoenix Sun. At Sunrise Stable, near Calgary, Harris and Phoenix learn dressage. This formal discipline is akin to ballet or figure skating, and puts horse and rider through movements derived from rangeland work and cavalry manoeuvres. For an urban college teacher, joining the horsey set is no small commitment. Boarding fees for Phoenix, excluding essentials like tack, veterinary care and trailer transportation to competitions, exceed $3,600 per year.

"BIG DOGS" TRANSFORM NATIVE SOCIETY

The horse has been a prized pillar of Western Canadian society since the first quarter of the 18th century. At least, this is the time of arrival established in Native memory and recorded by European explorer David Thompson, when he spent the winter of 1787-88 in a Peigan camp. Thompson's host, Saukamappee (Young Man or Boy), at age 75 to 80, could remember the tribe's first sight of a horse and why the animal instantly became as hotly desired as any of the European trade goods that also reached the plains at the time.

"We had more guns and iron-headed arrows than before," Saukamappee told Thompson. "But our enemies, the Snake (Shoshone) Indians and their allies, had Misstutim — big dogs, that is, horses — on which they rode, swift as the deer. They dashed at the Peigan and with stone pukamoggan (war clubs), knocked them on the head." The Peigan "thus lost several of their best men. This news we did not well comprehend and it alarmed us, for we had no idea of horses and could not make out what they were."

On a hunting raid south into Shoshone territory, west of the Rockies in what eventually became Washington and Oregon, the original Western Canadians had their first good look. "We were anxious to see a horse of which we had heard so much," said Saukamappee. "At last, as the leaves were falling, we heard one was killed by an arrow shot into his belly (as his Shoshone rider fled). Numbers of us went to see him. We all admired him. He put us in mind of a stag that had lost his horns. We did not know what name to give him. But as he was a slave to man, like the dog, which carried our things, he was named the Big Dog."

By the time Thompson penetrated the Canadian Plains, at the dawn of the 19th century, the horse had transformed Native society from pedestrian hunting clans into wide-ranging warrior confederacies. Stealing rivals' horses, rounding up wild ones and trading favourites were rites of passage to manhood, marriage, wealth, status and tribal leadership. Thompson recorded that horsemanship came as naturally as walking to Plains Natives, at almost as early an age. And that was no trifle. "Their walk is erect, light and easy, and may be said to be graceful," the explorer noted. "When on the plains in company with white men, the erect walk of the Indian is shown to great advantage. The Indian with his arms folded in his robe seems to glide over the ground; and the white people, seldom in an erect posture . . . swayed from right to left, and some waved their arms as if to saw a passage through the air. I have often been vexed at the comparison."

HORSEMANSHIP AND THE WEST

Nearly a century after Thompson's arrival, Colonel James Macleod of the North-West Mounted Police paid aboriginal horsemen high compliments by ruefully drawing a sharp contrast between the performance of the Natives and of Europeans transplanted to the plains. In 1878, still smarting from severe horse losses during the NWMP's Great March West four years earlier, Macleod submitted a plan to Ottawa suggesting that at least half the force's manpower should ride in wagons. He wrote, "To make our men effective to fight on horseback against such enemies as we might meet in the North-West, they would have to be engaged as children and made to ride every day till they grew up."

Gabriel Dumont, Métis war chief of the 1885 Riel Rebellion, described skills that Macleod and the Mounties would have faced if Louis Riel, the Rebellion's leader, had let his plains fighters wage the guerrilla warfare they learned from infancy. These skills were evident not only in the riders, but also in their horses. "Once I killed a Blackfoot when I was fighting for the Cree," 65-year-old Dumont reminisced in 1902. ". . . I chased him just like a buffalo. When I caught up to him I stuck the barrel of my rifle in his reins and fired. He fell forward onto the neck of my horse. At full gallop, the surprise made my mount rear violently and almost throw me off backwards. The Blackfoot pony stayed right beside me. I passed my leg over the neck of my horse and jumped to the ground, catching the riderless pony's bridle." Dumont did not brag. He talked just as candidly of enemies who had creased him with bullets and war clubs. He spoke as if he considered such horseback acrobatics to be routine for Plains Natives who lived into old age.

Natives often documented their history through pictographic memoirs inscribed on chiefs' ceremonial buffalo robes. These pictures recorded a free-wheeling, often violent lifestyle, with the horse at its centre. The Mounties held the clearest, most celebrated robe, that of Kainaiwa chief Crop Eared Wolf, under lock and key in a museum at their Regina headquarters for 50 years, until federal Solicitor-General Herb Gray returned it to the Kainaiwa in their southern Alberta capital at Standoff. He did this as a goodwill gesture on September 22, 1995, the 118th anniversary of Treaty Seven.

As depicted on this ceremonial robe, horses starred in three of five coups scored by Crop Eared Wolf, an upwardly mobile

16

young plainsman earning his stature as a revered chief. He stole a horse from Sioux warriors and, at a cost of gunshot wounds to himself and the animal, led it through their lines into a Kainaiwa raiding camp beside the Missouri River in the Yellow Stone Valley. On a swift dark horse beside the Belly River, 19 miles (30 km) from the site where the Mounties built Fort Macleod, he shot a Cree in a running fight and captured three horses and two saddles. He killed a member of the Crow in the enemy's own lodge and took away a scalp, four axes and a blanket. Near the Cypress Hills straddling southern Saskatchewan and Alberta, Crop Eared Wolf's war party vanquished a Cree band. It cost him a bullet wound in the leg that crippled him for life, but he stayed formidable on horseback. He rode on to steal a horse and mule from the Sioux in open country, then performed one of the ultimate feats in the plains lexicon of bravery and daring. He stole a horse from the doorstep of a tribal enemy by cutting a rope fastened to a pole inside a Sioux teepee.

Chief Crop Eared Wolf, who survived plains rough-housing to die of old age in 1913, straddled two eras. His coups belong to a brawling frontier period that followed the close of the American Civil War in 1865. For a dozen years, until Treaty Seven established land ownership, order, liquor prohibition and the rule of the Mounties (as judges, as well as police), the Canadian Plains were a no-man's land and virtually an appendage of the American frontier. The only way into the country was west by steamboat and up the Missouri to the end of navigable channels at Fort Benton in Montana, near today's Great Falls. The next leg was north on the Whoop-Up Trail — a horse and wagon route named for the principal item of commerce, alcohol.

When the NWMP arrived in 1874, the party faded fast, leaving few traces except for a handful of colourful place names, like Fort Whoop-Up near today's Lethbridge. The liquor business, a target of strict prohibition legislation, hid under counters and behind a system of permits which officially tolerated alcohol only for medicinal purposes. Just as Crop Eared Wolf became a tribal statesman revered for peaceful defence of treaty rights, celebrated whiskey traders like Lafayette French turned respectable. With O.H. Smith, French founded the OH Ranch. Peers likewise reincarnated themselves as ranchers, storekeepers and freighters, delivering supplies to the Mounties, Indian reserves and towns that sprang up overnight. The red-coated police stood out as the most visible of many other rapid developments that overpowered the wilderness. Among these were Confederation in 1867; the transfer of 'title to the West' from the British Hudson's Bay Company to Canada in 1870; grazing-lease grants that set off a ranching boom as soon as Indian treaties opened up land; construction of the Canadian Pacific Railway in the mid-1880s; and, finally, with

THE BARREL RACER

The majority of contestants in rodeo are men, but women also make a valuable contribution to the sport. Never welcome in the male sanctity of the rodeo arena, women have created their own place by sheer audacity and persistence, as well as courage and individual skill. Barrel racing, a test of horsemanship, training and skill, is the main event for women.

the advance of the railway west, waves of homesteaders lured by the Canadian government's offer of free land.

HORSES VERSUS TRACTORS . . . A PHILOSOPHICAL TUG OF WAR

Through all the changes in the West, the horse thrived. The horse population of Alberta, Saskatchewan and Manitoba peaked in 1921 at 2.5 million, while the human population was just over 1.9 million. With 2.5 million horses, the three western provinces held 70 percent of the Canadian total of 3.45 million head. Although the number of horses in the West fell by nearly half over the next 15 years, it was unclear even in the mid-1930s whether the tractor would ultimately dominate the plains completely.

A Depression-era survey of agriculture in the West stated that, after early inroads by tractors, the region showed signs of reverting back to the horse. *Agricultural Progress on the Prairie Frontier* (MacMillan; Toronto: 1936) reported that the tractor had evolved from its clumsy origins into a compact, efficient and reliable machine. Yet, the experts also found that the smart money — easily spotted as the homesteads that survived the Dirty 30s — refused to rely entirely on tractors, except for the biggest farms with the most favourable, flattest terrain. The farmer who kept using horses became an agricultural version of the wily, fast and adaptable warriors on the 19th-century plains. Mechanization and tractors spelled changes for the course of settlement and lifestyles. But with horses, Westerners stayed in command of where and how they used the land, especially since horses can function on any type of terrain. "The number of horses can be adjusted to farming on the mountainside or the plain; to the prairie or the woodland; to the market garden or the bonanza farm; to the dairy farm or the chicken ranch. The tractor is not so adaptable."

As workers, horses continue to be rated as unbeatable by even the best modern tractors in rough, steep and slippery terrain. "A good draft horse will outpull a 25-horsepower tractor," boasts Phil Gisler, Francis Gardner's top hand and horse trainer. Gisler decided that the mechanized family farm was not for him after his first few youthful tastes of working ranch cattle on horseback. "Horses are designed to pull. They're built for traction. They don't have wheels to spin." He and Gardner can think of no animal or machine more capable of the work on their hilly cattle spread, which runs to over 30 miles (50 km) of climbing and descending every day.

Francis Gardner belongs to a strong minority who still refuse to surrender entirely to mechanization. That minority is growing. In the short-grass country of eastern Alberta and western Saskatchewan, where more than half the original homesteads failed in some areas, farmers are going back to horseback ranching after parking their tractors and seeding the land with native grasses. The

COWBOY JOHN WARE

The cowboy is a product of his environment and work. Hard, lean and tough, he has many of the qualities of the range he rides. It's gritty work herding cattle in gale force winds and harsh winter storms.

resistance to a complete takeover by machinery is strongest in Alberta, where less than ten percent of Canada's human population owns at least 130,000 horses, or more than one-third of the national total. Alberta Agriculture's horse industry branch has estimated that six in ten farms in the province have horses. Far from all are just kept around for children to ride.

HORSE SENSE . . . AND A SPECIAL PARTNERSHIP

Phil Gisler's opinion of horses is straight to the point. "That's royal transportation," he says, adding that the more experience a person has with horses, the more respect that person has for them. "It's as if they're specially designed for people. Whatever you do on a horse, they react to it. Exactly what you give on a horse, you get exactly out of it. I don't know any other animal that does that." Good trainers — and neighbours pay Gisler and Mount Sentinel Ranch high compliments by hiring them as horse educators — start with a premise that they are dealing with intelligence. "They know all the movements. You can't really teach a horse anything. It's just a matter of how to get them to respond. The horse teaches a guy. Most horses we call dumb have been mistreated. They just act for their own self-defense. They don't lie to you," says Gisler.

A ranch owner will pay a premium for a top hand sensitive enough to understand the equine brain. Gardner acknowledges Gisler's horse sense as a rare talent. For Gisler, the relationship is a partnership, rather than master and slave. "Breaking — it's not the proper word. You get him used to people. The first time you get on, you let him do what he wants. Then you work on patterns of movement. Horses respond to your body language. They focus on pressure points (like knees, reins and bit). You always leave a door open for him so he can go. You make that the direction you want him to go. A horse always takes the easy way. You make it your way."

After a lifetime of earning a livelihood on horseback, Francis Gardner draws a sharp distinction between trained and "seasoned" stock. "Arena-trained" falls far short of satisfying the qualifications for a working cattle horse, valued from $6,000 to $8,000 on markets that recognize the scarcity of the genuine article. An arena-trained horse only knows all the moves in the most favourable environment. A seasoned one can be trusted to do it all without stumbling or panicking on rough, hilly terrain full of natural hazards like gopher holes and hornets. Step one towards seasoning is often to give an arena-trained horse a chance to learn not to hurt itself or its rider, just by turning it loose to run in the hills on its own for a few months.

Gardner adds, "Most people say a horse is a tool, something you use up until you are done. That's the way I grew up. To see them as intelligent, intellectual animals and deal with them on that level — it's quite a gift. You need to be humble to realize how

21

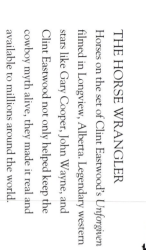

THE HORSE WRANGLER

Horses on the set of Clint Eastwood's *Unforgiven* filmed in Longview, Alberta. Legendary western stars like Gary Cooper, John Wayne, and Clint Eastwood not only helped keep the cowboy myth alive, they made it real and available to millions around the world.

dumb you really are. They're a brilliant animal. You pick a spot in your mind and a seasoned horse will know where you are going. It's a lot to do with how you think and feel about things. Horses will respond. They don't miss a bit, not anything."

Newcomers to ranching who give a relationship with a horse a chance to develop come to the same conclusions. Gardner's California-born wife, Bonnie, repeated the feat of early plains women by learning to live with drastic changes, ranging from the harsher climate to the high economic risks of earning a livelihood off notoriously unreliable livestock and markets. She fell in love with foothills ranching the old-fashioned way, on horseback.

To reach the same conclusions, the sporting set just takes different paths, on lighter English gear and in more formal clothing. Paula Harris glows with enthusiasm as she grooms Phoenix Sun, with brushes worn like gloves, into immaculate condition for a dressage workout. "They're really sentient animals. They feel everything. They pick up all the signals. If you're afraid, they are too. If you're tense, they are too. I had a fall. He stood there with his head down. He didn't like the situation either. It scared him, too. Horses are sensitive and understanding. They're intelligent. People say they've got such small brains — well, they're dumb like foxes. He knows my voice. There is a bond. It's really, really close."

The Business of Horses

One of the West's hardiest family businesses stands out as a living monument to the endurance of the horse, its trappings and the lifestyle that goes with it. MacLean Auction Mart, in Calgary's Inglewood community, lies a stroll away from the junction of the Bow and Elbow Rivers, where the NWMP founded Calgary by erecting a fort in 1875. Located in the heart of the inner-city, the market is one of the few premises that has made it intact through all the booms, busts and construction stampedes that have repeatedly razed and rebuilt the community. The building was already well established as a livery stable in the oldest photograph, dated 1909, that owner Gary MacLean has been able to find. He heads the third generation of MacLeans to run the market, while also making a go of a mixed cattle and farming operation east of Calgary.

On his auctioneer's perch, he works a few steps away from a spot that serves as a reminder of a darker side to his business, from the horse and buggy era. The firm's founder, grandfather Alex, died on the sales barn floor by breaking his neck in a fall head-first through a trap door. A casualty of one of the many occupational hazards of working with horses and livestock, he caught his hand in a hay bale being thrown down from the barn loft.

Almost in the shadow of Calgary's oil company skyscrapers, denim-clad auction patrons congregate to breathe the rich barn smells, inspect the merchandise and bid against one another. They pack the arena for monthly Friday-night horse and tack auctions, plus weekly Saturday sales of other livestock and ranching or farming gear. Gary MacLean described the business as busier than ever in late 1995. "There's more uses for horses than ever. There are more things to do, especially in the recreational line — in competitions like cattle penning and amateur team roping and so forth. Broke and registered horses'll run you $2,000 and up. A halter-broke colt goes for $700 to $1,500." The bidding can run high, even though this ring is neither the high end of the equine business nor intended to be. Slaughter-house buyers lurk in the arena but often go away empty-handed.

AND THE FUN OF HORSES

Westerners place about $300 million in bets every year at race tracks in Alberta, Saskatchewan and Manitoba. Albertans lead the pack by wagering more than $230 million, or 12 percent of the Canadian total of $1.9 billion. Alberta's total also tops British Columbia's $200 million, and trails only the more heavily populated Quebec's $311 million and Ontario's $1 billion.

Race tracks only scratch the surface of the West's continuing love affair with the horse. Country rodeos and the Calgary Stampede, with its annual gate admission of over a million enthusiasts, remain mainstays of the western hospitality industry. Rooted in 19th-century horseplay and professional rivalries among cowhands, and packaged by spiritual heirs to wild west shows, the western fairs preserve direct links to the frontier past. Vaudeville star Guy Weadick developed the formula for the first Stampede in 1912, and it has been going strong ever since. At big civic fairs, rodeo is just one element among a growing list of attractions, including agricultural, industrial, performing-arts, and crafts exhibitions. But it is the rodeo competition with horses and livestock that puts the snap, sizzle and tradition into the fairs.

Confirmation that the horse casts a magic spell across all walks of life in the West comes from a relatively new phenomenon — the Spruce Meadows centre for international Olympic-style equestrian events like dressage and show-jumping.

The centre, beside the southern tip of Calgary, had modest beginnings. Ron and Marg Southern started it in 1975, for tournaments among their children and peers from other families with a taste for refined riding. Neighbour Anne French recalls the early days. "It was just a field with an ATCO trailer on it. The first year, there were 10 or 15 of us clapping to the victory ride." The equestrian centre's flagship event, its Masters Tournament, has mushroomed since 1976 from a neighbourhood weekend

24

outing for 1,400 into a fixture on the international circuit, drawing crowds of 300,000 or more. In 1995, contenders competed for $2.6 million in prize money.

Spruce Meadows' three main tournaments — the National, North American and Masters — kick $107.5 million a year into Alberta's economy and provide a basis for over 1,200 jobs in the hospitality industry. At the centre's 1993 recreation and competition horse auction, buyers laid out $430,000 for 107 Quarter horses, Appaloosas, Pintos, Paints, Morgans, Arabians and sport horses. Top prices at the auctions have ranged as high as $26,000 for proven show-jumpers, and as low as $2,000 for recreational mounts.

The more refined forms of horse sport are not new to the West. Although rodeo completely stole the spotlight for decades, Spruce Meadows eventually emerged as a reminder that not all horseback events are rough and tumble, and that gentler tastes had arrived with the first ranchers. Many Canadian frontier families were anything but rubes. Early pioneers included strong contingents from the well-educated upper and officer classes of the British Empire.

Gymkhanas, a variation on the Spruce Meadows theme, started in the 1890s, along with polo and hunting. Millarville, in the heart of ranching country south of Calgary, had a race track by 1905. And polo teams of ranchers and NWMP officers from the Fort Macleod, Pincher Creek and Standoff districts competed successfully from Montana to Eastern Canada. British-style horseback hunting even took place on the plains, with hounds and all the other formal trappings, except for foxes. They were too scarce. The western chase settled for coyotes.

These politer forms of horseplay crossed gender barriers and broke the monotony for homemakers. Horseback outings made up the bright side of pioneer experiences, and were something for ranch women like Moira O'Neill to write home about. "In some ways, winter is quite as pleasant as summer; and when one can get coyote hunting, summer is not to be named in the same breath with it. The fun we had coyote hunting with our friends last Christmas-time passed all."

Whether mounted for work, play, competition, cultural revivals or political demonstrations, horses continue to have no peer in the minds of Westerners. It only takes a few rides on a decent mount to rediscover the joys of plains life known to many early homesteaders.

SPIRITUAL AFFINITY ACROSS CULTURES

The Siksika, reviving skills and trails of their ancestors, say no other sensation comes close to the finish of a 185-mile week

25

on horseback. Especially since the ride ends at a teepee encampment at Castle Junction, set up as a Native children's day camp and summer school. Riders who complete the marathon trek from Blackfoot Crossing to the mountains four times are deemed to attain a state of grace. It entitles them to membership in a sacred tribal society. Al Red Crow describes the experience as an emotional high that no amount of saddle soreness can diminish. "It's pretty special. It chokes you up when you ride in there, hear the music and see the elders and children."

The ultimate joys, on working and sport horses alike, often occur in solitude, as experiences shared by only the animals and their riders. A feeling of completeness in a partnership with another form of intelligence can flood through Francis Gardner at the tail end of a hard day of tricky, hazardous manoeuvring to herd cattle across high ridges and steep valleys. "It's not to show off. It's not a peer group thing. I've noticed that a lot of people who take pride in horsemanship do it by themselves. It's a form of living in wisdom that's ancient. It goes back as far as there have been people and horses. Each generation rediscovers that beauty and wisdom for itself."

Paula Harris, too, has had her special moments, in partnership with her horse. From her radically different starting points in Central Canada and with a city career, she has reached a point of spiritual affinity with Red Crow, Gardner and Gisler. She rates even a successful urban life as missing a vital dimension, unless it can be enriched by frequently climbing on a horse. "They're a wonderful beast. Riding is so different from work. It's relaxation. It keeps me fit. Phoenix Sun makes me work. He makes me try to feel more and think less. You have to feel where your body is. Your body has to take over."

She has to settle for trails between sprawling suburban real-estate developments, but on the right horse they can be open enough for a taste of the glory felt by the rancher among his remote ridges. "When it works, it's just a beautiful feeling. You learn to relax and let it happen — like one warm day when we'd been out riding. Sunset came. A coyote came along the trail, saw us, stepped aside, sat and watched us. Phoenix looked at him a moment, then gave his head a shake and jingled his bit. The coyote ran off into the sunset. It's too damn beautiful."

■

■

■

26

A PERFECT TEAM

INDIANS AND HORSES were a perfect match from the moment horses appeared on the Northwestern Plains. Observers of the day noted they worked so well together that horse and rider often seemed as one. While most tribal legends about horses, their origins and their power are considered folklore by modern Native societies, the notion that Natives and horses have a natural bond and an enduring understanding still exists today. For proof, descendants of the buffalo hunters need only look as far as their constables on patrol, like Rod Scout of the Siksika Nation Police Service.

Out on the beat 62 miles (100 km) east of Calgary, Scout has the efficient air and equipment of a thoroughly contemporary lawman, with a blue uniform, leather jacket, sunglasses, radio-dispatched cruiser, 40-calibre Beretta pistol, and training comparable to his urban peers. But in his personal life, another, older side came out when it was time to become a husband and father. In asking for his bride's hand, he presented his father-in-law with four Quarter horses — and good ones, he recalls with emphasis. This was no commercial transaction. Rather than a bride price, the gesture established him as an upstanding citizen of the society he serves — a man of respect, substance and generosity.

This high regard for horses began with the earliest encounters of man and horse on the Northwestern Plains. Plains Natives revered horses for the way they retained devotion and stature while all else changed around them, and they credited divine intervention for these remarkable qualities. Stories and legends sprang up and were passed down through the generations. All tribal legends on the origin of horses had common central themes. The horse came from sky or water spirits — the most potent, revered and feared figures in the plains pantheon — and passed on touches of divine power to the rider.

In the first of three principal versions of the horse's arrival, a wise man brought the horse back from a quest for better means with which to hunt. He crossed the mountains to the end of the earth, where he met the Great Sky God of Thunder. In exchange for a woman and a white buffalo robe, he fetched the stallions and mares which became the founders of the plains herds.

The second version of the horse's arrival was that a poor boy caught the ear of the Old Man of the Lake by praying aloud for a secret power to better himself. The Old Man sent his son to test the youth. Was he smart enough to take good advice?

When the Old Man of the Lake offered a choice of any animal in the place, the youth passed the test by obeying instructions to pick a humble mallard and ducklings. As the boy led the ducks to land, obeying further strict instructions not to look back, they shed their feathers and turned into horses.

In the third story, Morning Star, son of the Sun, heard a chief's wife wishing upon a star for a happier life. Morning Star came to earth to marry the woman and gave her the horse. She went to the heavens with Morning Star, and when she became homesick, her heavenly husband let her return to earth. She came back with a son she had borne by Morning Star. But her first husband tired of the new boy and mistreated him severely. In reply to more prayers for help from the woman, Morning Star gave the horse to an older son, borne by the woman before her sojourn in the heavens. This older son had proven himself to be responsible, kind, tolerant, brave and all-in-all, more deserving to be chief. With the power of the horse came power to kill the evil old chief and take over the leadership. In doing so, the woman's son also kept a great promise to the community, which was, "You need never walk any more."

Early explorers and anthropologists who recorded plains culture at its height viewed the Natives' oral traditions as symbols akin to the flattering portraits of their own European monarchs. With this view, they assigned the horse no less practical importance than did the legends.

By the time descendants of the 15th- and 16th-century Spanish explorers' horses reached the Northwestern Plains, generations of adaptation had hardened them into agile, wiry, spirited and long-winded types that became known as Indian ponies or cayuses. These were not disparaging terms. They were bywords for compact, fast and intelligent allies. Saukamappee, a warrior in his 70s who sheltered David Thompson in a Peigan lodge for the winter of 1787-88, told the exploring fur trader he was a married man by the time the tribe had its first experience with horses. This dates the horse's arrival on the Northwestern Plains — Alberta, Saskatchewan and Montana — as no earlier than the second quarter of the 18th century.

Within two or three generations, acquisition of the horse transformed plains society by ending its millennia-old pedestrian era with new means of travel, hunting, recreation, making war, transporting freight, and measuring wealth. Far longer distances suddenly became easier to cover. Quick, exciting chases replaced ancient, slow "surround" methods of stalking buffalo in teams on foot, and driving them into brush corrals or over cliffs. Hunters continued to use bows and lances, in sizes scaled down to be handy on a galloping animal, almost until the end of the herds. Muzzle-loading guns were too awkward and slow. Repeating rifles and pistols

THE BUFFALO HUNTER

only began reaching Natives in the 1870s, when chiefs like the Blackfoot Confederacy's Crowfoot, seeing an end to the buffalo, resigned themselves to signing treaties that made them ranchers or farmers.

With horses, Native warfare changed. Infantry-style battles, with lines using long bows and heavy shields, were transformed into cavalry clashes, which began as massed charges and ended in one-on-one duels with lances and clubs. Fighting in the form of small raiding parties may also have become more frequent, to the point of almost continuous combat.

Horses were always in scarce supply. Stealing from rival tribes rapidly became a combination blood sport and respected route to personal wealth, distinction as a warrior, and tribal leadership. This tradition, born in the mid-1700s, became one of the sorest points and worst causes of conflict with traders, police, ranchers and settlers who began arriving on the plains a century later with less sense of adventure about their property.

Unlike Europeans, Natives mounted horses from the right. Anthropologists described right-hand mounting as a possible case of long-distance cultural "diffusion" from the early Spanish explorers and settlers. They may have introduced Natives to the horse by employing them as grooms.

Whatever the circumstances, the match between Natives and horses could not have been a better one. A war or hunting horse ultimately became an extension of its owner, decked out in a rich plains lexicon of paint, symbols and sometimes head-dresses. Strong colours, symbols recalling victories, and sacred circles depicting connection with all the universe, including the Creator, decorated man and horse alike, to portray a team united in courage, intelligence, power and spiritual strength.

■

■

■

THE BEAVER MAN

HORSE AND TRAPPER SHUDDER as a wall of raging snow, broken trees and deadly rocks catapults down the steep valley wall. The pair barely escapes death. Deep in the Rocky Mountains of the Canadian West, a tentacle of the fur trade empire searches for pelts. There are no beaver in these mountains, but still the beaver man plods on. Over the divide he pushes into the Kootenay and Columbia river valleys. There he finds furs and the Natives who trap them. He and his packhorse link the beaver ponds in the western reaches of Canada to the wealthy of the Old World. In England and Europe, beaver pelts end up as top hats on the heads of stylish men and as stoles around the shoulders of fancy women.

The story of fur is as old as human habitation. Fur is warm. Pockets of air trapped in each hair offer unparalleled insulation. Thin in July, thick in February, animals grow and slough it off as needed. Thousands of years ago, Natives learned to make traps and harvest fur-bearing animals with spears. They used stone knives to separate the pelts from the bodies, and deer brains to treat hides, cleaning and preserving them for use as clothing. Beaver, muskrat, deer, elk, bear and buffalo all surrendered their hides to keep their two-footed predators warm.

Living in close communion with nature, Native hunters and gatherers made use of almost every part of the wild animals they stalked and trapped. Beaver, muskrat, and smaller animals provided hides that had to be pieced together. Ungulates such as buffalo, moose, elk and deer provided large skins, suitable for clothing, tents, canoes and many other things. These animals provided sustenance for North America's aboriginal people as well as bones for tools.

The first Europeans, seeking Asia and India, arrived in the 15th century at the shores of North America. They found their maritime route blocked by a continent with treasures of its own. Fish in unprecedented abundance off the coast of the New World supplied European tables for centuries. While on land drying the catch, the fishermen met Natives and exchanged trinkets and other goods for interesting furs and articles made of bone. Although most transplanted Europeans continued to rely on familiar food and clothing from home, some adapted to the harsh conditions in the New World by dressing in furs and eating meals with their hosts. Slowly, trading partnerships developed from these relationships.

On the second of May, 1670, the "Governor and the Company of Adventurers of England Trading into Hudson Bay" received a charter from the King of England to reap the natural harvests of the bountiful land which drained into Hudson Bay. The Hudson's Bay Company began its life as little more than a shipping company. Its trading posts, located at strategic points around Hudson Bay, collected fur from Natives. In exchange, "The Bay" supplied metal implements such as pots, pans, knives and rifles. As trade grew, tobacco, rum, cloth and many other manufactured items filled the ships that sailed west from British ports. Summer was a time of rejoicing as voyageurs arrived with furs in large canoes, and later, in York boats. Dancing, visiting, drinking and gambling went on continually until the ships left for England and the long trail back to the frontier beckoned.

For the remainder of the year, life was often hard. Winters were darker, colder and harsher than most Europeans could imagine. In the forts around Hudson Bay, many went mad during the long winter nights, with little heat and almost no entertainment. Others committed suicide. Still others sought the comfort of "country wives," Native women whose cultural tradition was to form relationships with other tribes.

Still further out in the uncharted new world, trappers struggled and slogged through miserable cold or slushy conditions, regularly making their rounds on interminable traplines. When wolves and other predators did not beat them to the catch, they extricated the frozen corpses, set the traps again, and staggered home. There, they thawed the stiff furs and cut them away from the bodies of the small animals. Hours of scraping, stretching and curing were necessary before a raw fur was ready for market. Even then, fur buyers might be days or weeks of travel away. Fur prices rose and fell with market demand, based on fickle European fashions. The cyclical nature of fur-bearing animal populations also added to the insecurity of life on the trapline.

And what of this beaver man, what was he doing in the mountains? Everywhere else, the fur trade conducted its business by highways of water, as most marketable fur lived along the rivers. Even the smallest streams were capable of moving product to market during spring floods. As generations passed, trappers wiped out fur resources in eastern and central North America, pushing the frontier to the farthest reaches of the rivers. At the headwaters of the mighty western rivers, even the most intrepid explorers, traders and trappers had to abandon their canoes and continue on horseback or foot.

The beaver men did not stop when they reached the wall of mountains called the Rockies. They pressed on through the high passes, challenging themselves and forcing the elements to make way for the fur trade. Through the early 1800s, explorers David Thompson, Alexander Mackenzie and Simon Fraser blazed routes through the mountains to the Columbia Department and

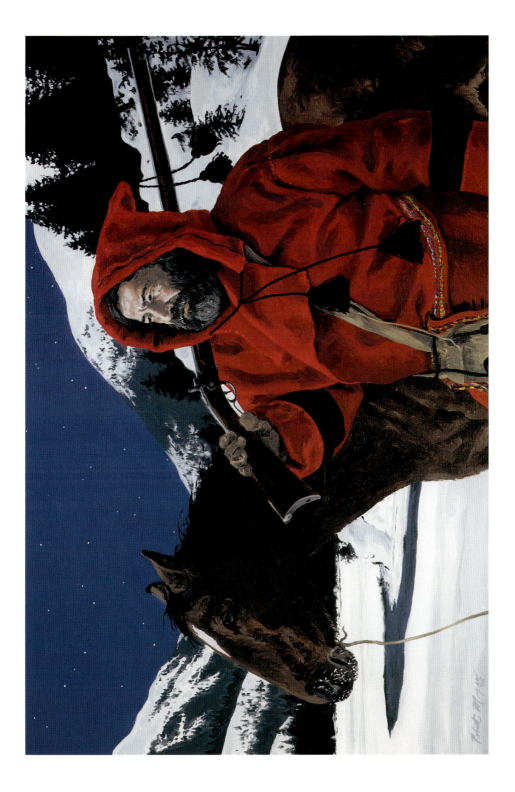

NIGHT WINDS

New Caledonia west of the continental divide. In this new furbearing territory, trade continued on horseback. Up dangerous valleys, through log-choked streambeds, over mountainous passes and wind-swept highlands, teams of packhorses moved furs and trade goods back and forth from the interior of British Columbia to the long water routes to Hudson Bay.

Before the country of Canada was born, it was the fur trade that drove exploration. The Hudson's Bay Company developed into more than a fur trading corporation. It held dominion over the entire North-West Territories, providing a lifeline to Europeans carving out the fur trade and a source of wondrous new tools and materials to the Natives. It took courage to extend the fur trade into unknown and mountainous territory as resources were trapped and hunted to near extinction across the Plains. An unlikely cross between a cowboy and a voyageur, the beaver man played a unique and important role in the development of the Canadian West.

■

■

■

34

THE RED RIVER CARTS

ON A JUNE DAY IN 1849, over 1,200 tall-wheeled carts headed out from the Red River community on the biggest bison hunt of Métis history. Westward they went, seeking their ultimate provider. They travelled for 12 hours each day and, after 19 days, they spotted the herd and put careful plans into action. More than 400 hunters on horseback awaited a signal and shout from the captain of the hunt. When it came, they rode slowly at first and then charged into the buffalo herd, stampeding them. They killed 1,375 animals the first day, shooting from the hip on the run, loading rifles from bags of powder and mouths full of shot. The best among them killed ten or twelve buffalo each. After the carnage of the hunt, the carts arrived. Women began processing the buffalo, cleaning the hides, making pemmican, drying jerky and feeding the hunters and children from the bountiful supply of fresh meat. For almost two months, the Métis pursued the buffalo. They returned on August 17, 1849 to the Red River community with 500 tons of meat and pemmican borne on Red River carts.

Within 50 short years, the buffalo were no more. One story jests that they heard the terrible noise of the screeching, clattering Red River carts and dove into gopher holes to escape the cacophony. Although the carts became part of the annual Métis hunt, they did not directly spell the end to the bison (or chase them underground). However, in the same way that the horse made travel easier on the prairies, the carts — and later the railway — made way for an advancing culture which put a gradual end to the bison and the traditional way of life of the Natives and Métis.

Some people collect belongings as proof of wealth, and build their comfort and security upon possessions. This characteristic makes them immobile. By contrast, the first inhabitants of North America never developed this tendency, as survival relied upon a nomadic way of life. They moved frequently during their annual round of activities, following game, visiting trading centres and joining relatives and friends for annual feasts and celebrations. Not surprisingly, they also sought moderate weather for their winter camps. This need for mobility prevented them from accumulating goods, simplifying their moves. In early times, they only took with them what they could carry on their backs and what their dogs could pull. Eventually, horses allowed them to carry more possessions, but it was the arrival of Europeans and the wheel which changed this way of life most profoundly.

35

The first carts in the Canadian West used solid wooden wheels, cut from the largest trees available. Derived from similar carts in Quebec and Europe, they quickly evolved in the Canadian West and skilled craftsmen built them using locally available materials. Early versions carried five times as much as a horse. With a payload of almost half a ton when pulled by an ox — less when harnessed to a pony or an old horse — the carts were the first vehicles to make trade routes viable on the prairies.

Later models boasted spoked wheels as tall as a man. Made by the Métis, descendants of French fur traders and Plains Indians, the Red River carts, as they were known, used no steel screws or nails, but rather wooden dowels for fastenings. Wet buffalo hide, stretched over large wheels, bound them tightly when the leather shrank. Design refinements included having the wheels fit inside the cart for river or lake crossings. But the most readily distinguishing characteristic of the Red River carts was the screeching noise they made as they rolled along. The noise came from the axles, which were run dry to prevent dust and dirt from collecting in grease and causing the wheels to seize.

Dry land was no place for the voyageur and his birch-bark canoe. Although rivers ran through the western plains, water levels dropped early in the summer and did not provide reliable navigation routes. Further north, the Churchill River system was a virtual highway for the fur trade. The Great Plains of the American and Canadian West waited for the railway to open them to a great influx of settlers.

Until the rails reached the West, rivers like the Mississippi and the Missouri transported merchandise to their headwaters in the American Northwest. From the shores of these rivers, ox-carts moved supplies north and west into the Canadian prairies as early as the 1830s. Regular cart service began in 1843 when Joseph Rolette began driving a small brigade of six carts from St. Paul, Minnesota to Fort Garry, near today's Winnipeg, Manitoba. By 1851, there were more than 100 carts on that route. The number rose to 600 by 1858 and peaked at 2,500 carts in 1869.

Trading links like this helped break the Hudson's Bay Company's stranglehold on commerce in the Canadian West. Unlike the steel tracks and trains that arrived in the 1870s, the Red River cart used indigenous materials. Trains needed massive financial investment and only ran on expensive track. Carts, by comparison, cost about $10 in 1849 and even less if built by the owner. More often than not, a Métis was in charge of the Red River cart brigade. The Métis were highly skilled in all aspects of nomadic life in the changing Canadian West of the 19th century. Their cart brigades quickly became common across the plains, shipping goods to trading posts and buffalo robes back to the closest water or rail link.

SCREECHING WHEELS

For a few short generations, Métis buffalo hunters and their Red River carts experienced this unique life. Because the carts allowed them to kill and transport more meat than they needed, they sold pemmican and buffalo hides or robes to traders and early white surveyors and settlers. Cash allowed them to purchase manufactured goods from Europe. Métis hero Gabriel Dumont, famous for his skills as a horseman, hunter and warrior, was a customer of "The Bay." In 1860, his purchases included cloth for women's clothing, red and green flannel, printed cloth, braid, ribbon, thimbles, needles, cord trousers, a black cloth vest, and silk and cotton handkerchiefs. He also bought flour, tea, soap, clasp knives and halter rings.

But the Métis way of life was destined to end. The increasing pace of settlement and the disappearance of the buffalo sealed their fate. Fearing for their future, the Métis dispatched Gabriel Dumont to Montana to fetch Louis Riel. On June 10, 1885, Riel returned from exile in Montana to Batoche, travelling with his family in a Red River cart — a symbol of a passing way of life. As the axles of the carts split the air with their nerve-wracking squeals, he crossed the border into Canada, instigating what became known as the Riel Rebellion. Within weeks, militia troops were sent west on the partially completed Canadian Pacific Railway line. As the rails replaced the Red River cart, the Rebellion was crushed, ending the traditional way of life of the Métis.

■

■

■

GREAT MARCH WEST

WHILE CANADA OFFICIALLY CAME INTO EXISTENCE in July 1867, its founding fathers, led by Sir John A. Macdonald, knew the fledgling country would not achieve true nationhood until the Canadian West was settled. In 1870, the Canadian government purchased the North-West Territories from the Hudson's Bay Company, and the process began, only to be derailed by the Red River Uprising in 1869-70. Although negotiations with Louis Riel and the Métis resulted in the formation of the Province of Manitoba, the event made it clear to Ottawa that Canada needed to enforce its sovereignty over the new territory.

In addition to these concerns, whiskey traders from the United States had invaded Canada, leaving violence and debauched and broken Natives in their path. The central government knew action had to be taken and in May 1873 The North-West Mounted Police Act was proclaimed.

But passage of the act didn't cause the force to be formed immediately. Mired in the "Pacific Scandal," Sir John A. Macdonald was trying to avoid the political fall-out from taking massive campaign contributions from American investors in the Canadian Pacific Railway. Six weeks after the proclamation of the act, a group of 30 American whiskey traders, posing as wolf hunters, crossed the 49th parallel and slaughtered 30 Assiniboine Indians. What became known as the Cypress Hills Massacre refocused political will and a police force was finally formed.

In late November, frost-bitten and weary from an arduous trek through early winter storms, the first 150 ill-equipped recruits arrived at Fort Garry, 20 miles (32 kms) north of Winnipeg. With less than 40 horses, many of them unbroken, training commenced. It was brutal work as many of the recruits had never been on a horse. Training went ahead in the thick of the harsh Manitoba winter, with the men sharing time on the horses and taking turns being bucked off onto the frozen ground.

In early 1874, Commissioner George Arthur French convinced the new Liberal government to purchase 250 more horses and recruit 200 more men. Soon after, John Poett was hired as veterinary surgeon, at a salary $200 per year higher than the men's doctor.

After the arrival of the new recruits and horses, on July 8, 1874 the "Great March West" began. Six Divisions of North-West Mounted Police, outfitted in the finest regalia to ever cross the Plains, led the expedition. White helmets, blazing red tunics, white gauntlets, high leather boots, gleaming braid and powerful sidearms made the men look like apparitions. On matching steeds, each Division rode mounts of a different colour: A Division on dark bays, B Division on dark browns, C Division on bright chestnuts, D Division on greys and buckskins, E Division on blacks and F Division on light bays. In total, 275 officers and men started across the wide ocean of grass.

One hundred head of cattle and almost 200 freight wagons and Red River carts accompanied the expedition, complete with two nine-pound field guns and two brass mortars. Mowing machines to cut hay, farm machinery, portable forges and mobile kitchens rounded out the equipment.

Strung out over ten miles (16 kms), the force was a commanding presence for the first few weeks. But slowly, reality set in. The recruits were poorly equipped and ill-trained for the conditions they found on the trail. Travelling close to the American border, the police passed through a drought ravaged land, scarred by wildfire. With temperatures as high as 90 Fahrenheit (30 Celsius), the stock and men suffered in the brutal heat of the barren plains. Slough water, when they could find it, was unappealing to the stock. Grazing was difficult, and in places, non-existent. Mosquitoes, horseflies, hail storms and grasshopper plagues of biblical proportions added extra misery to the hardships.

Soon, animals slowed, dropped and died while the men looked on, helpless to change their fate. Scorchingly hot prairie winds parched the men and remaining animals, and filled their eyes and lungs with dust. At one point, wildfire broke out and threatened to roast them alive.

Food supplies ran short. The men bought pemmican when they could find it, and went without food when they couldn't. Fear of Indian attacks caused them to sleep in their clothes. Finally, almost completely desperate, they came upon a herd of buffalo and ate well from the kill of fresh meat.

Well beyond their normal range, Métis scouts guided the force to its destination at the junction of the South Saskatchewan and Bow Rivers. Weary and nearly beaten by the journey, they arrived September 11, 1874. The police had hoped to find a whiskey post at the site and arrest some traders. But finding no evidence of either, they retreated to the Sweetgrass Hills on September 19. New reconnaissance finally took them to the whiskey post at the confluence of the Bow and St. Mary's Rivers, south of the modern city of Lethbridge. The post was deserted.

Despite the horrors of the Great March West, the Mounties had a job to do. The police officers would each serve a short

THE HORSE ARTILLERY

term, two or three years, and then stay on as settlers in the new West and be on call as a reserve force if necessary. Compared to the 30,000 Native inhabitants who occupied the West, the force of "not more than 300 men," as the NWMP Act proclaimed, was small. But, all of the officers were sworn as justices of the peace and the commissioner had the powers of a magistrate. Despite its small size, the force was at least equipped with the legal authority to mete out quick and decisive punishment to lawbreakers.

Fear of violence in the West was well founded. As hunters killed off the last of the great herds of buffalo, unscrupulous traders arrived with alcohol. Natives, unfamiliar with whiskey, fell prey to its vile hold. Liquor ruined many Natives, demoralized families, and rendered once-proud hunters unable to provide for their wives and children. Natives were driven to desperation, and violence and conflict erupted with whiskey traders. Marauding bands of outlaw, horse-stealing Natives also threatened the order of the West. Settlers would not move to the frontier if they feared for their lives, and populating the West was critical to Canada's agenda. The arrival of the NWMP and the reputation of Canadians as law-abiding citizens helped calm the fears. This was not the open wild west of American fame. The Canadian North-West would be based on the rule of law.

In retrospect, while the Great March West itself was nearly a disaster, the final result was a true success. Building on a Canadian tradition of cooperation with the Natives, the Mounties reinforced law and order in the Canadian West. By the time they reached the abandoned whiskey posts within sight of the Rocky Mountains, the raw recruits had become skilled horsemen. The mounted force grew up with the settlement of the Canadian West and created a proud tradition of a peaceful Canadian frontier.

■

■

■

MUTUAL RESPECT
THE NWMP AND SITTING BULL

THE NWMP HAD BEEN IN THE SADDLE barely four years in May of 1877, when Superintendent James Walsh met Tatanka Iyotanka, Chief Sitting Bull of the Sioux Nation. Eleven months earlier, Sitting Bull and his warriors had crushed General George Armstrong Custer and the U.S. Seventh Cavalry at Little Big Horn. With the United States Army hot on his heels panting for revenge, Sitting Bull had little choice but to flee to Canada.

With the chief came a following which rapidly grew into one of the largest plains aboriginal encampments ever recorded, 5,000 Indians with 15,000 horses. Sitting Bull's arrival posed a test which became a formative experience for the fledgling national police force. Could the NWMP — with a total of just 329 men and 315 horses, half the size of the Seventh Cavalry — keep order? More importantly, could the NWMP do the job within its mandate to be a moral rather than a brute force?

With their masters in Ottawa counselling the use of kid gloves, the NWMP moved their headquarters from Fort Macleod to Fort Walsh and fended off American demands for Sitting Bull, until he left of his own free will in the autumn of 1881.

The NWMP made a deal with Sitting Bull and the Sioux premised on two conditions. The Sioux had to obey the laws of the land where they squatted, and they had to refrain from staging raids across the border. The deal worked and the NWMP even gave them hunting ammunition and food handouts in emergencies.

The Native leadership kept this bargain, restraining young warriors at considerable cost in prestige when small NWMP units made examples of horse thieves by performing dramatic arrests in crowded, near-explosive teepee villages.

Respecting the police was a fair price to pay in the eyes of Sitting Bull, a celebrated philosopher, song writer and leader of the largest plains aboriginal nation. The NWMP's tolerance allowed him to stay one of the last "free" Indians, as in the 19th century called those who resisted becoming a party to the American pattern of treaty making and gifts. This pattern also included forced sales of land or even outright repudiation of commitments, culminating in wars on "hostiles" who resisted.

Sitting Bull's arrival posed a dilemma to a young Canada, united just ten years earlier with the express purpose of saving the northern half of the continent for civilization as a loyal Dominion of the British Empire. "Would the heirs to the original redcoats "surrender power to the Americans?" Sitting Bull asked. "And would the original inhabitants be turned over too?" As the Sioux flocked across the new international border, they asserted their moral claim to be in Canada. They showed the Mounties medals stamped with King George III's portrait, proving their ancestors had served on the British side in the American Revolution and the War of 1812.

Canadian authorities had abundant political reasons to pay attention to the Natives. The NWMP had a higher priority assignment than fighting refugees from the turbulent American West. The Mounties had a mandate to win trust among Canadian Plains Natives to provide a foundation for treaties and reservations in preparation for settlers and construction of the transcontinental railroad.

The humane peace policy of the NWMP appealed to personal instincts among the officers. Superintendent Walsh belonged to an international school of thought which believed Indians should be treated in a fatherly fashion, firmly but with kindness and instruction, rather than the lash.

In the winter of 1876-77, Walsh showed his sympathy when he led a squad to meet an advance guard of the Sioux. He reported, "The warriors were silent, and solemn, the mothers' hearts were beating; the maidens' eyes were dim and war had made the children forget how to play."

Sitting Bull and the Sioux sensed Walsh's attitude and responded in kind. They gave the NWMP officer respectful names, White Forehead and Long Lance. The bond even survived a famous spat. Walsh, strained by hardships among Canadian Natives as well as the political and policing demands made on him in mid-1879, bodily ejected Sitting Bull from his home. The chief had come asking for tea and tobacco on the heels of a complaint by a rancher alleging horse thefts by the Sioux. After a tense but brief armed confrontation between police and Sioux riflemen, Sitting Bull shrugged off the personal slight, even though it was a serious matter in a culture which puts a premium on "face", to the extreme of surviving the touching of enemies or rivals to be as good as defeating or killing them.

Besides satisfying their consciences, the NWMP took pride in doing a cleaner job of keeping the peace than American authorities. The Mounties' commander, Commissioner James Macleod, documented the sorry state of race relations in the U.S. by the last quarter of the 19th century. In a report on the Sioux encampment, written to his chief in Ottawa, Interior Minister David Mills, Macleod wrote, "I was actually asked the other day by an American who has settled here if we had the same law here as on

IN THE LAND OF THE MOUNTED POLICE

the other side, and if he was justified in shooting any Indian who approached his camp after being warned not to advance. I am satisfied such a rule is not necessary in dealing fairly with the worst of Indians, and that any necessity there might be for its adoption arose from the illegal intrusion and wrong doings of the whites."

The four years Sitting Bull spent in Canada gave the Sioux Nation its last taste of the golden age of living by hunting on horseback. The stay ended only because the high population concentration accelerated destruction of the last buffalo herds. As meat vanished, the Sioux trickled back across the border. Homesick and faced with starvation, they accepted much harsher conditions, dictated by the U.S. government, for being allowed to survive on American soil. As well as surrendering all horses, guns and bullets, they underwent virtual incarceration on reservations, often on the poorest land left over after miners and settlers took the best.

When he left Canada in 1881, Sitting Bull travelled far out of his way to pay a last call on Walsh, who had been transferred northeast to Fort Qu'Appelle near the flatlands which eventually became Regina. It is a testament to the mutual respect and admiration the two men had for each other.

In a private letter on the occasion of Sitting Bull's death — he was shot by an American Indian reserve policeman — Walsh described the chief as "misrepresented. He was not the bloodthirsty man reports made him out to be. He asked for nothing but justice. He was kind of heart. He was not dishonest. He was truthful. He loved his people and was glad to give his hand in friendship to any man who was honest with him. He experienced so much treachery that he did not know who to trust."

■
■
■

PEACE WITH HONOUR

ONLY A MODEST CAIRN, ringed by a faded white picket fence and reached by unsigned gravel roads, marks the spot where two civilizations met on horseback on September 17, 1877, to create a new society. The resemblance to a grave is no coincidence. Blackfoot Crossing, a vast natural amphitheatre in the valley of the Bow River 62 miles (100 km) east of Calgary, evokes mourning and yearning among heirs to both sides who participated in the peace agreement, officially recorded as Treaty Seven.

Soon after the treaty was signed, settlers crowded into the region and shunted Natives aside with a potent blend of residential (boarding) schools, religion, charity, prohibitions and regulations. The United Church of Canada eventually made a formal public apology for its role in this forced assimilation. And the federal government has repeatedly tried to undo its share in the aftermath by attempting to replace the Indian Act with a negotiated system of self-government. The apologies and invitations to negotiate have been gracefully accepted by Native leaders, but they know that what they need is rebuilding, which can only be led by aging elders, the preservers of plains aboriginal culture and language.

At one of many reserve events intended to correct side effects of the treaty's later interpretation as a surrender, Tom Crane Bear — a prominent elder of the Siksika (Blackfoot) Nation — voiced the Natives' perspective 118 years after the signing. "We lost a lot of our traditional values through this big change. The big change was a big hurt. The healing is getting back to our basic under-standing of who we are. We are lost. For the healing to begin, you have to believe in yourself and who you are. It's a huge task."

If only, sigh both sides — if only the just intentions of the treaty's makers had come true. For there was no doubt at the time, or in historical verdicts since, that the peace made at Blackfoot Crossing was truly a gentlemen's agreement between eminently civilized leaders.

A three-day ride northeast from Fort Macleod brought the North-West Mounted Police to the site of the signing in 1877. At the head of the column of 80 Mounties rode a scarlet-clad Colonel James Macleod, who believed in the Canadian heritage of British ideals, of one strict but fair law, uniform for all, regardless of colour or creed. Macleod escorted, advised and vouched for the Canadian government's senior treaty commissioner, the like-minded David Laird. Laird was lieutenant-governor of the North-West

Territories, which included Alberta and Saskatchewan until they became provinces in 1905. The NWMP picked Jerry Potts, one of the most celebrated plainsmen of the day, to act as interpreter. Potts, the son of a mixed marriage, had earned respect on both sides of the era's rigid racial fence as a winner on Native battlefields and peerless guide of explorers.

Back in 1874, Macleod had been obliged to prove himself to the plains tribes as soon as the Mounties arrived at his name-sake fort on the Oldman River. Missionary John McDougall, who doubled as an envoy for the Canadian government from his base among the Stoney Nation at Morley, had prepared the Plains Indians for the NWMP's arrival by spreading promises of protection against liquor and exploitation. The Blackfoot tested Macleod by laying complaints against a whiskey trading post. The NWMP promptly arrested two bootleggers from the United States, swiftly jailing one trader, fining the other, destroying their liquor and confiscating their post's weapons and trade profits. Macleod established early the legend of the Mountie who always gets his man, and endeared the force to Natives in the process. He immediately rounded up Americans responsible for a border fight over horses with the Assiniboine, a one-sided affair in 1873 that became internationally notorious as the Cypress Hills Massacre and helped stimulate the creation of the NWMP. He pursued the gunmen into the U.S. so vigorously that he was arrested by a Montana sheriff and had to fight for his own freedom in an American court. The culprits were eventually freed, after a trial in Winnipeg, for lack of strictly legal evidence against them. Macleod repeatedly delivered similar performances as the NWMP's commander, and eventually became one of Western Canada's first magistrates.

Leadership of the tribes at Blackfoot Crossing belonged by moral force to Crowfoot, a legendary figure and plains version of Winston Churchill. Crowfoot is revered to this day. Formally, he was chief of only the Siksika, one-third of the Blackfoot Confederacy, which also included the Blood, Peigan, and the allied Tsuu T'ina (Sarcee). But all deferred to his favourable judgements of Macleod, Laird and their promises on behalf of the government in Ottawa. The treaty commissioners likewise deferred to Crowfoot's sense of the occasion. He chose the riverside site for its pedigree as a meeting place and battlefield among plains equals, rather than leading his people to a police fort, where the event would have felt like submission. Impressed by Crowfoot, and coaxed by McDougall, the Stoney set aside ancient rivalry with the Blackfoot clans to make Treaty Seven a complete package, by including their territory along the foothills of the Rocky Mountains.

Crowfoot had earned his stature. Starting in his early teens, he delivered stellar performances in 19 battles, and endured six wounds. He also stood out as a seasoned campaigner who learned how to keep his men alive by refraining from fighting against bad

48

BLACKFOOT CROSSING

odds. Plains conflicts were tough teachers. Crowfoot lost his father and eldest son to failed raids.

By 1874, Crowfoot could see overwhelming odds against his people surviving at all, unless some accommodation could be made for forces invading the plains. From the north and east came old rivals like the Cree, Assiniboine and Métis, pushed by swelling tides of settlement from Canada and Europe. From the south came the Sioux, driven by the blue-coated U.S. cavalry, as well as silent but even mightier killers — smallpox, diphtheria and liquor. To the west lay the end of the plains against an all but impenetrable mountain wall. And all around, Crowfoot told McDougall, the buffalo lay dying as the last spasms of frenzied hunting exterminated the Plains Natives' source of food, clothing and shelter.

Crowfoot made up his mind in early 1877. He expressed his philosophy of survival through peace with honour by publicly rejecting Sitting Bull's invitations to mount a last fight to the finish against the U.S. Army. The Army wished to avenge the Sioux destruction, in June, 1876, of General George Armstrong Custer and the 7th Cavalry at the Little Big Horn in nearby Montana. Crowfoot declared, "To rise, there must be an object. To rebel, there must be a wrong done. To do either, we should know how it would benefit us. We do not wish for war. We have nothing to gain, but we know people make money by war on Indians and these people want war. Let the government know we favour peace and want it. I have done." He followed the same principles in rejecting invitations to participate in the Riel Rebellion eight years later.

At Blackfoot Crossing, Crowfoot led the Natives in accepting Treaty Seven, saying, "I trust the Great Spirit will put into their breasts to be good people, also into the minds of the men, women and children of future generations. The advice given to me and my people has proven to be good. If the police had not come to this country, where would we all be now? Bad men and whiskey were killing us so fast that very few of us would have been alive today. The Mounted Police have protected us as the feathers of the bird protect it from the frosts of winter."

The Indians ceded 50,000 square miles (130,000 km²) — all of southern Alberta, including the sites of Calgary, Lethbridge and Medicine Hat — in exchange for 1,470 square miles (3,800 km²) of reserves, cattle, grain, coaching in their use, and annual "treaty money" of $5 apiece for all and $25 for chiefs. But the plains tribes had no cultural concept of real estate as property, and little knowledge of money or agriculture. Above all, they followed Crowfoot's example in having faith that they were bargaining for peace and respect in place of American-style bloodbaths and displacements.

Macleod affirmed the great chief's interpretation in a closing address, stating, "Your chiefs know what I have said to them

50

during these past three years — that nothing would be taken away from you without your consent. You have witnessed the truth of this today. I also told you that the Mounted Police were your friends, that they would never wrong you or see you wronged in any way. You see this is true also. The Mounted Police will continue to befriend you and will always be glad to see you. In turn, you must keep the Great Mother's (Queen Victoria's) laws."

In eleven days of speeches, ceremony and sometimes high-spirited partying, the Blackfoot Crossing deliberations became the last great treaty of the North American Plains and brought a dramatic finish to the West as a wild place without property ownership. The assembly filled the six square miles (15 km^2) of graceful meadows by the Bow with painted lodges, sweetly-scented campfires, rich cooking smells, throbbing drums, mesmerizing chants, the neighing of prized horses and the barking of dogs used as beasts of burden by plains societies. Warriors, hunters, chiefs, their multiple wives and numerous children rubbed shoulders with Mounties and some of the officers' wives. While Native women and children walked, warriors raced about on horseback, staging mock charges, including volleys of gunfire into the sky at climaxes of the pageantry. The NWMP preserved their reputation by not batting an eye, and upheld the sense of occasion by wearing their best-dress red coats and polished leather at all times. The treaty was endorsed by 4,392 Natives, who received $52,954 in cash, including signing bonuses.

The site rapidly emptied as snow squalls coincided with the end of the ceremonies. Within months, the presents, bonuses and high spirits faded as the hard realities Crowfoot had seen coming arrived. The buffalo thinned out fast. Crowfoot led the Siksika-Blackfoot on a long last hunt, roving deep into the U.S. They struggled back north on foot — starving, and stripped of their horses by raiders and whiskey traders — to start learning to live on the reserve in 1881. The Blood, Peigan, Tsuu T'ina and Stoney likewise settled down to adapt to relative confinement.

The Canadian Plains Natives have not disappeared or given up on reaping the great promise of equal partnership in western society which lured them into Treaty Seven. That promise is finally being realized, gradually, through the work of wise and persistent Native leaders and elders in conjunction with the Canadian government. One of the results of this work is the opening of a public safety centre for the Siksika Nation, made possible by the reinterpretation of Treaty Seven. A mid-1995 ceremony in honour of the opening was attended by Native leaders and elders, Mounties in scarlet and senior government officials. Even the Crazy Dog Society came to bless the building, making their first public appearance in Siksika Chief Strater Crowfoot's memory. The Society's traditional role was akin to policing, and their title "Crazy" described how vigorous and self-sacrificing its adherents intended to be in protecting women and children. Crane Bear said that, properly endowed with this spirit, the 1995 vision of the treaty and the new safety centre will work the same way. "This is the beginning of the healing process we're always talking about . . . . All employees will be Siksika, from the judges to the janitors. It's just going to take time."

Crane Bear of the Siksika Nation only now talks freely about the "big hurt" which followed its greatest leader's decision to trust outsiders. And his community has finally begun to see a happy ending ahead.

■

■

■

THOMAS WILSON

TRAIL BLAZER OF THE ROCKIES

BUILDING THE CPR took men of character, men of strength and men who could face the toughest of challenges without blinking an eye. Major A.B. Rogers was such a man. Charged with surveying a route for Prime Minister John A. Macdonald's transcontinental railroad through the great Canadian Rocky Mountains, Rogers was renowned for his fierceness and discipline. Legend has it this crusty old surveyor lived off plugs of chewing tobacco and rashers of bacon. Tough as railway spikes, he demanded obedience and fealty from the men who worked for him.

One of those earliest employees was Thomas Edmund Wilson, a man who devoted his life to exploring and showcasing the Rocky Mountains. Soon after the railway was completed, Rogers left the Rocky Mountains. But Wilson stayed on, earning a reputation as the best packer and hunting guide in the West.

Born in 1859 and raised in Ontario, Wilson had come west in 1880 to answer the call of the recently created North-West Mounted Police. By train, steamboat and horse, he travelled to his NWMP posting at Fort Walsh. However, it soon became clear that police work failed to hold his interest, so he left the force, travelled south to Fort Benton and began an adventure-filled career.

Early summer of 1881 found Wilson riding herd on 80 pack ponies from Fort Benton, Montana north into the unsettled Canadian West. After successfully fording the flooding Oldman River, he arrived at Fort Macleod and made friends with Dr. G.M. Dawson, who was commissioned to survey the mountains for the Canadian government. Crossing flooded creeks and rivers, fearing for their horses and worried by Natives, they finally arrived safely at Fort Calgary on July 3, 1881.

That night, a riot broke out. Men spilled from their tents, grabbing rifles, preparing for the worst. Fear of Natives made many men yell, "Indians! Indians!" and shoot into the dark hoping to frighten off the suspected hordes. Fortunately, no one was injured in the shoot-up. Finally, an American confessed he had started it all, blasting off his rifle and hollering to celebrate the Fourth of July, as was the custom south of the border. The Canadians were not amused.

Days later, Wilson met the infamous surveyor Major Rogers at The Gap, where the Bow River makes its escape from the Rockies just east of Canmore. Rogers rode up to Wilson, his monstrous side whiskers billowing in the breeze, and promptly took charge of his new men and supplies. For the most part, Rogers' greeting of Wilson is unprintable, but Wilson remembered it as "a wonderful exhibition of scientific cussing." It was working for Rogers that inspired young Wilson's life-long love affair with the mountains.

Learning to accommodate clients is difficult for every guide, but Wilson learned from the toughest of all, Major Rogers. Harsh of manner and remarkably foul of tongue, the surveyor was quickly hated by all the new men. When he asked for a volunteer, none came forward. Finally, Wilson raised his hand and his education began. Wilson quickly learned Rogers' bravado was a disguise. Beneath the rough exterior lay a human being, harshly driven to find a route for the rails through tough mountain passes.

As Rogers sought his route, Wilson laid out the life-line pack-train trail from Calgary. Across the remaining plains, over the foothills, in through The Gap, and along the Bow River and Vermilion Lakes, the trail brought much-needed provisions to the surveyors. Wilson chose the camping spots and each night made a crude shelter by stretching tarps over a double row of saddles. Wrapped in thin blankets, the packers slept as best they could in all weather. During the day, they ate cold bannock, sowbelly or bacon, and drank a bit of tea. Under harsh and difficult conditions, the skills of the mountain men increased with each trip.

Not one to wait around for adventure, Wilson headed back into the mountains in 1882. While packing supplies for CPR construction crews, a Stoney Native named Gold Seeker mentioned a "lake of the little fishes." Intrigued, Wilson followed the Native up a valley to discover a stunning mountain scene. A lake the colour of turquoise beneath a suspended glacier greeted the riders. Wilson called it Emerald Lake, only to have it renamed Lake Louise by CPR map makers. Later that summer, while following a herd of wandering horses, the mountain man discovered the picturesque valley which includes what is known today as Emerald Lake.

That summer of 1882, Wilson almost starved to death proving that Howse Pass was not a viable railway alternative to Kicking Horse Pass. Alone and running short of food, he scouted the alternative route on foot. The ravines were full of fallen timber and the trail was exceptionally poor. Finally, after almost breaking his leg many times, he stumbled down the banks of the Columbia River, without food and almost incoherent. Major Rogers, worried sick and in a rare show of compassion, greeted him like a long lost son. Still in the service of the railway, Wilson also helped make peace with the Natives as the track sped across the prairies.

Wilson later resigned from the railway and went into the timber business. He also made time to prospect for metals at Field, British Columbia. A boom mining town called Silver City, near Castle Mountain, also attracted his attention.

54

ALONG THE VERMILIONS

But soon, he answered a different call, moving to live in a small cabin at the Lake Louise railway siding.

In 1885, Wilson joined Major Steele's Scouts and helped handle the general unrest in the Native and Métis population caused by the Riel Rebellion. In November of the same year, he attended the driving of the golden last spike at Craigellachie, B.C., to commemorate the completion of the Canadian Pacific Railway from Montreal to Vancouver.

It was also in 1885 that Wilson married Rev. John McDougall's niece, Minnie McDougall. They soon settled down in Morley, in the Alberta foothills east of Canmore. In 1887, his skills as a guide took him back deep into the mountains with his first big game hunting party.

By 1893, the Wilson family had moved to Banff to be near the work the guide loved so deeply. He outfitted hunting and mountaineering clients for many years. As an original member of the Canadian Alpine Club, he also started the Banff Indian Days celebration in 1894, an annual event which continues today. Always interested in helping to promote tourism, Wilson was also part of the group which organized the Trail Riders of the Canadian Rockies in 1924.

Before he died in 1933, the grand old mountain man had trained most of the early Banff guides, who in turn introduced people from around the world to the mountains in Canada's first national park. He was a packer to tobacco-spitting old Major Rogers, a mountain man of international reputation, and an organizer of associations and events which brought the majesty of the mountains to the world. Tom Wilson, a consummate guide, richly deserves his title as the Trail Blazer of the Canadian Rockies.

■

■

■

LOUIS RIEL
GUARDIAN OF THE METIS CULTURE

WITH A WILD FURY, the armed Métis galloped over the prairies on their spirited horses. A cloud of dust followed them across the plains till they reached the river. The men vaulted off their mounts and descended on an unsuspecting Canadian government survey party on October 11, 1869. "Get out and take that survey chain with you," they commanded. "This is not your land." Shoulder to shoulder with André Nault, they defied the legal force of the Canadian government. The surveyors retreated. The time had come for a unique Western Canadian people to make their stand. Their leader was Louis Riel.

In 1869, the Hudson's Bay Company sold the North-West Territories to Canada. However, neither the Company nor the government of Canada had consulted with the inhabitants of the Red River colony. The Métis worried about becoming part of Canada. Concerned that immigrants from Central Canada would upset the balance of power, the Métis feared for their French language and Catholic religion. As settlers began migrating to the new frontier, their land purchases came into conflict with the traditional ways of Natives and Métis.

Finally, in the last days of 1869, Métis leader Louis Riel acted. He shut down a Canadian survey party, created a National Committee of the Métis of Red River, and prevented William McDougall, the first lieutenant-governor of the North-West Territories, from taking up his post.

Riel's group then seized Upper Fort Garry without firing a shot, owing to the fierce reputation of Métis buffalo hunters and warriors. Riel established a provisional government. Although most Westerners supported the Métis leader, Riel's actions did not go locally unchallenged. Thomas Scott, an Ontario Orangeman, a Protestant and an intense British loyalist, was an outspoken and violent opponent. Finally, Riel's government court-martialled and executed him. Riel had thought this execution would prove the power of the provisional government and force the Canadian government into serious negotiations. While Scott's murder, as it was termed in Central Canada, may have moved up negotiations, the negative repercussions far outweighed any possible advantage. English Canadians were outraged when they learned Riel's government had tried and executed Scott hastily. Worse yet, the trial was conducted in French, and Scott did not understand the language.

Unable to get an armed force to the West before the summer, and fearful the Métis would encourage Americans to come north, Ottawa began negotiations. It proclaimed the Manitoba Act in May, 1870, granting the Métis voting, educational and land rights. However, the Métis victory was largely hollow, as it applied only to a small province, barely one hundred square miles (160 km²). The remainder of the North-West Territories continued under the total control of the central government in Ottawa.

Riel fled Manitoba just as a Canadian expeditionary force under the command of Colonel Grant Wolseley arrived to restore Ottawa's vision of law and order to the West. The Métis leader was suspicious of the amnesty he had been offered by the Canadian government. He spent most of the next fifteen years in Montana.

With order seemingly established in the West, hundreds of immigrant settlers began pouring into the new Eden, putting additional pressures on the Métis population. Plagues of grasshoppers in 1873 and 1874 took the Métis' crops, and many Métis sold their land in Manitoba. Most of them moved west, trying to regain their traditional lifestyles by hunting the few remaining buffalo.

In what is now Saskatchewan and Alberta, the construction of the Canadian Pacific Railway in the early 1880s attracted still more settlers. Others came west on American railroads and then north by stage or cart. Progress came quickly and unrest grew as whites, Natives and Métis attempted to live together in a climate of change.

By 1884, discontent had reached a peak. Famed buffalo hunter and warrior Gabriel Dumont was dispatched to Montana for Louis Riel, the father of the Province of Manitoba. During Riel's time in the United States, he had married and begun raising a family. But the 40-year-old man had also become mentally unstable, even spending some time in Quebec's Beauport Lunatic Asylum, haunted by the need to save the Métis Nation from encroaching settlers.

Legend surrounded Riel's leadership. The Métis believed their hero could save them again. Together they would make a last stand and force Ottawa to bend to the will of the West. They planned to seize land, establish a government and once again embarrass Prime Minister Macdonald into respecting the Métis cause. Their future depended on their charismatic hero.

Arriving in Batoche on a Red River cart, a symbol of the Métis way of life, Riel attempted to repeat his success of 1870. He sent a list of requests for rights to Ottawa in December, 1884. Prime Minister Sir John A. Macdonald, still smarting from Riel's strategic victory in 1870, ignored the basic food needs of the Métis and Natives until it was too late. On March 19, 1885, Riel and Dumont commandeered the store at Batoche, took hostages and declared a Métis provisional government.

The Canadian government responded with an armed force. At the Battle of Duck Lake, Superintendent L.F. Crozier of the

RIEL VISITS BATOCHE

North-West Mounted Police and 100 men escaped with 12 deaths and as many wounded. Five Métis lost their lives. The prime minister then sent 800 additional soldiers west under the command of Major General Frederick Dobson Middleton. Travelling over the partially completed Canadian Pacific Railway, the hastily gathered troops arrived two weeks later. Volunteer white settlers in the West also came forward. Sam Steele, John "Kootenai" Brown and other western heroes provided leadership for the western militia. Soon 8,000 soldiers stood ready to support the government in Ottawa against the Métis and Natives.

Riel, still confident negotiations would take place, restrained Dumont from implementing the guerrilla tactics that would almost certainly have sent the reinforcements scattering. More troops arrived as Riel continued to stall. Finally, with incredibly superior resources, Middleton attacked the Métis at Batoche on May 9, 1885. Outnumbered and outgunned, the Métis held on for three days, firing nail fragments when they ran out of ammunition. Although they fought valiantly from ingeniously constructed rifle pits, the Métis eventually surrendered. On May 15, Riel turned himself in.

While French Canadians and Métis hailed Riel as a hero, English Canadians considered him a scoundrel and a traitor. The leader of the Métis Nation was charged with disloyalty to the Queen. Despite being an American citizen, Riel was tried under British law before a European-born jury. Insanity was his only possible defence, but his eloquent testimony in support of the Métis cause sealed his fate. On November 16, 1885, the trap door opened beneath his feet and Louis Riel dropped to the end of the hangman's rope.

As offspring of European voyageurs and Natives, the Métis carved out a unique place for themselves in Canadian history. Their hero, Louis Riel, stood up to the Canadian government and defended the special way of life of his people. Today a larger-than-life statue of Riel stands outside the Manitoba Legislature, reminding all of the special promises made to the Métis. Riel will be remembered as the father of Manitoba and as the cherished leader of a unique Canadian people, the Métis.

■ ■ ■

COCHRANE'S MEGA-RANCH

ALBERTA HAS A REPUTATION for thinking big. A century before promoters coined the word megaproject for the province's mammoth oilsands developments, its early ranchers thought big. That spirit lives on in the name of Cochrane, a town 25 miles (40 km) west of downtown Calgary which proclaims its roots with a Western Heritage Centre and a larger-than-life statue of a mounted cowboy on a hilltop.

Senator Matthew Cochrane, son of an Irish immigrant, thought and acted big in all departments of life. He first made his fortune in Central Canada in the shoe and leather business, after leaving his family's farm in Quebec's Compton County, an area celebrated for fine livestock breeding. Although Cochrane never ran for office or even openly took part in politics, he gave the Conservative party enough support that in 1872 Canada's first prime minister, Sir John A. Macdonald, appointed Cochrane to the Senate.

As a confidant of Sir John A. Macdonald's inner circle, Cochrane had ready access to the results of missions dispatched by the government to explore the country's newly-acquired North-West Territories. He glimpsed the vision which inspired pioneer ranchers as early as 1870, in a status report written by W.F. Butler, a captain borrowed from the British army. Between dry official accounts of geography, demography and political conditions – including early warning signs of the 1885 Riel Rebellion – Butler's report captured the excitement of the West and became the essence of his international best-seller, *The Great Lone Land*.

After the national government had followed Butler's recommendations for creating the North-West Mounted Police and making treaties with the Natives, Cochrane wasted little time. Butler's report had inspired many prospective ranchers, and Ottawa was still preparing the policy for grazing leases in mid-1880 when Cochrane presented the prime minister with a pitch for a big western ranch. The plan called for a spread that could go beyond raising beef for Natives, settlers and the NWMP. It would serve as a breeding station for stocking the entire frontier, by supplying other entrepreneurs with livestock. By late 1881, Cochrane and associates formed a company, picked the spot where his namesake town now stands, secured 300 square miles (770 km²) of leases and started collecting cattle.

Cochrane had little time for critics, and refused to let even expert skepticism slow him down. While shopping for land in 1881, he met one of the most experienced roamers of the plains and Rocky Mountains, and heard strong reasons to think twice. John "Kootenai" Brown told the aspiring rancher it was wrong to think cattle could just step in where the buffalo used to tread. The old hand had seen lessons learned the hard way on the American range. Brown warned Cochrane the climate was unreliable. It was not safe to rely on warm Chinook winds to shorten winter cold snaps and keep the snow cover light. The animals were different, too. Buffalo extracted all the nutrition from plains grasses by eating the plants down to the roots. Buffalo kept moving constantly, travelling hundreds of miles every year to find pastures. The wild herds were tough enough to travel into frigid north winds, if that was what it took to reach new grazing. By buffalo standards, cattle were inefficient browsers and delicate. Cattle turned their backs to the wind and wandered wherever it might push them. Brown urged Cochrane to at least stockpile hay for ranch livestock.

Cochrane barely paused. He had already set his plans in motion. He teamed up with another pioneer cattle outfit, the Bar U, to import 136 British Hereford, Angus and Shorthorn bulls, plus a clutch of Clydesdale work horses. While the prize bulls made their way across the Atlantic, then up the Missouri to the end of navigation at Fort Benton in Montana, Cochrane's agents scoured the northwestern U.S. for healthy range cattle. Summer ran out by the time they assembled about 6,700 animals near Fort Benton, at a cost of a life when a trail hand drowned in a river crossing.

The biggest long-distance cattle drive ever mounted by a Western Canadian ranch became a grim forced march for more than 200 miles (320 km) from northern Montana to the waiting ranch site. Thirty cowhands strained themselves and a 300-horse remuda, or herd of remounts, to set a record pace. They "tincanned" and "slickered" — used noisemakers and flapped rain gear — to goad the main herd of steers into making as much as 18 miles (29 km) a day, double normal pace. Cows and calves struggled along behind for 14 miles (22 km) every day. Stragglers died or were traded for butter, milk, tea and stronger drink by the "drag" crew at the tail of the mammoth column. The survivors paused for a head count at the Bow River in October, then marched the last 25 miles (40 km) to the ranch just in time to beat the onset of winter. Exhausted, weakened animals died in the hundreds when the cold arrived on their heels.

Cochrane, unshaken by the harsh first experience and warnings by range veterans that it could have been much worse, had the exercise repeated the following year with nearly 5,000 cattle. But winter arrived earlier in 1882. A September snowstorm and exhaustion stranded the herd for a month at Fish Creek, about 12 miles (20 km) from the Bow, and a long trek from civilization.

ARRIVAL OF THE SENATOR'S RAREBREEDS

By hiring less weary local cattle and cowhands to break trail, the Cochrane outfit reached the ranch in late fall. The September storm turned out to be just the first in a series. Cold snaps sent cattle drifting with the wind throughout the Calgary region and far beyond. By spring, an estimated 3,000 animals had died.

With two strikes against him, Cochrane looked for greener pastures. He found some near where he had encountered Brown, about 125 miles (200 km) south around Belly River, and east of present-day Waterton Lakes National Park. The chastened rancher rapidly secured leases for almost as much land as his original spread. Much of the cattle operation rapidly moved to the new location. It proved to be an excellent choice. Warm Chinook winds blew east across the Rocky Mountains, abating the cold and making grazing easier by melting snow, while the woods and brush of the foothills provided protection from the blowing winds of harsh winter storms. The kinder location and helpful neighbours allowed the Cochrane outfit to emerge as one of the stronger survivors from a string of hard winters that reached a climax in 1886-87, when severe storms devastated ranches in more exposed places across the American and Canadian West.

At its peak in the late 1880s, the Cochrane organization ran more than 13,000 cattle and the biggest sheep herd in Western Canada on land holdings of 334,500 acres (1,354 km²). But the drive to keep the operation going died with its founder in 1903, and Cochrane's heirs gradually relinquished the holdings.

Was this pioneer megaproject a success? Negative verdicts have been heard, especially from contemporaries who saw animals die in legions and who ran afoul of the giant outfit in disputes over land, stock and branding. But the mega-ranch also groomed province builders like A.E. Cross and James Walker, whose entrepreneurial and civic leadership put Calgary on the map as a business capital and home of the Stampede. Perhaps they owed their success to their mega-ranch experience with the man who taught them to think big.

■

■

■

PRAIRIE SEA

WITH THE ROCKY MOUNTAINS for a scenic backdrop, only greenhorns mistook events like driving cattle across the Bow River for exciting horseplay. It was a frequent sight in the Calgary area during the late 19th century. But crossing swift, cold waters with temperamental livestock — and in heavy work clothing liable to drag even a good swimmer under after a spill – stood out as one of the riskiest parts of range work. Last crossings were occasions for relief and celebration. These events left memories which endured for generations. A testament to such memories is Robert Magee's *The Last Crossing*, commissioned during Calgary's centennial in 1994 by rancher Angus Sparrow's descendants, who wanted to commemorate his achievements in founding ranches near Strathmore, Cochrane and Midnapore.

When it came to moving cattle, there was no shame in avoiding rivers. John Ware, a cattleman renowned for personal courage and plains know-how, enhanced his esteem among his peers by finding a way to stay out of the Bow. He defied a Calgary bylaw and smuggled a herd across the fledgling city's only bridge over the river, in the middle of a June night in 1900.

Sir William Francis Butler, the British soldier, explorer and author whose writing set off the era's ranching boom, described Western Canada's harsh realities while at the same time cloaking the land in glamour. In his international best-selling adventure-travel classic, *The Great Lone Land*, he gave a sensational account of an 1870 intelligence-gathering mission across the West, which he performed for the government of Sir John A. Macdonald. At his most stirring, the eloquent pundit compared the plains to the sea, with imagery that inspired a generation of pioneers and fortune seekers. Butler declared that 16th-century navigators had the right idea with maps which portrayed the interior of North America as an inland sea and northwest passage to China. "The geographers of that period erred only in the description of the ocean which they placed in the central continent, for an ocean there is, and an ocean through which men seek the treasures of Cathay, even in our own times. But the ocean is one of grass, and the shores are the crests of mountain ranges, and the dark pine forests of sub-Arctic regions. The great ocean itself does not present more infinite variety . . . One saw here the world as it had taken shape and form from the hands of the Creator."

The seasoned traveller in Butler tempered the image of a vast new Eden with equally graphic reminders that this sea of land, like those of water, had perils — not the least of which included unpredictable water and weather. He told how a beloved mount, Blackie, carried him 560 miles (900 km) west from Winnipeg in two weeks, only to die a horrible death in the North Saskatchewan River on the third day of mutual torment trying to ford it. The compact stallion fell through late-autumn ice and could not be pulled out. Butler had to shoot the animal rather than let him die slowly of exhaustion and drowning: "He looked at me so imploringly that my hand shook and trembled . . . . It may have been very foolish, perhaps, for poor Blackie was only a horse, but for all that I went back to camp and, sitting down in the snow, cried like a child."

Plenty more tears watered the plains in the years after Butler's trek, and not just over lost horses. Drowning became a common hazard as ranchers surged into the plains decades ahead of road and bridge builders. A cowhand drowned in 1881 ushering in the cattle boom that stocked the vast Cochrane spread. No amount of experience could overcome the hazard. Not even the North-West Mounted Police, seasoned by the range since 1874, proved to be immune. Constable Alfred Perry drowned on patrol in 1889 while trying to swim his horse across a river. Ranching and Native communities recorded four drownings in swollen southern Alberta rivers in 1897, a year recorded as a once-in-a-century round of plains floods not repeated until 1995.

Horses and cowboys alike routinely took risks on cattle drives because they had to keep herds together and moving. The dangers showed in periodic tragedies like the 1894 drowning of veteran hand Saul Blackburn of the Walrond Ranche. The Walrond (known today as the Waldron) was one of the best and most successful outfits, and was organized by prominent veterinarian Duncan McEachran. Blackburn and his mount perished while comrades looked on in helpless horror. It had been his turn to take on a standard, dangerous part of the routine during river crossings. To keep cattle moving across a ford by preventing them from following instincts to drift with the current, cowhands had to take up positions downstream of the herds. Blackburn and his mount took an unlucky step too far off the shallows. The current bowled over both horse and rider into swift, deep water.

The plains sea also had a peril akin to the ocean's pirates. While the NWMP had a right to boast that it kept the Canadian frontier tame compared to the American West, there was no shortage of police work. Stamping out horse and cattle thievery kept the force busy for its first 20 years.

In the beginning, Natives took much of the blame for livestock theft. Their pre-settlement culture, after all, put a high value on horse theft as a measure of a warrior's talent and bravery. But the police spotlight shifted to others by the end of the 19th century. A nest of buccaneers from the Sweetgrass Hills along the border between Alberta and Montana was openly stealing

66

THE LAST CROSSING

livestock, with swaggering threats to shoot anyone or burn down the homestead of any family that tried to stop them. The gang was reputed to be an outlaw remnant of Louis Riel's 1885 rebel forces, and it terrorized settlers in both jurisdictions for years. In a mid-1890s dawn raid, the NWMP stole the gang's horses and emptied their guns. When the gang came looking for their missing mounts, the NWMP arrested them all.

It took until 1903 to stamp out a plains variation of privateering, a cruel form of "finders keepers, losers weepers." It had been born along the notoriously lawless boundary between Texas and Mexico, and then imported with the first herds of longhorns that reached Western Canada from the United States. Unbranded cattle were called mavericks and considered fair game for whomever had the might to take them, no matter where they might be found. The old maverick doctrine evolved into a might-is-right shortcut for covering big ranches' expenses. Cowhands collected and sold any unbranded cattle they came across, to pay food and other bills incurred by roundups.

A.L. Sifton, a former justice for the North-West Territories and later Alberta's second premier, staged a highly effective one-man crusade to impose more civilized property rights on the cattle ranges. Prison sentences for rustling climbed to 10 years, and the practice rapidly died down. Sifton, acting on complaints by two German-speaking homesteaders, whose cows were scooped up as mavericks, fired a shot across the bows of cattle associations in Maple Creek and Medicine Hat. He symbolically convicted all the association members of theft, and made them return the cows. The maverick tradition died. At the same time, the last imports of lean, half-wild longhorns from the U.S. petered out, and beefier, more docile and more profitable breeds, such as Herefords and Shorthorns, took full possession of the great Canadian prairie sea.

■

■

■

PARADISE LOST

THE RELATIONSHIP BETWEEN WESTERN CANADA and the weather has not always been a love affair. When pioneer ranchers tell stories about the old days, the weather figures prominently as one of the most difficult obstacles to their survival. A word that often comes up is "eveners," brutal winters long and cold enough to knock out all but the best at coping with the frontier. Eveners strip away advantages of size, wealth, birth, education and political connections. The term was coined by veterans of the first Western Canadian ranches, who started from scratch in the 1870s. They described an evener as a full year of hardship, with a summer drought coming on the heels of a bitter winter.

By 1902, the feeling that some natural selection in ranching was overdue was voiced in the *Fort Macleod Gazette*, which stated, "There are old-timers who do not look with favour upon the many new range ventures. To them, the country wants what is called an evener." This was a reaction to increasing settlement in the area.

To lure settlers, the Canadian Pacific Railway and Ottawa's Ministry of the Interior mounted a marathon propaganda campaign in the United States, Britain and across Europe, as far east as the Ukraine. A blizzard of pamphlets spread two boasts. The first, that a vast empty land — literally advertised as an "ocean" — could be had for free, provided homesteaders took advantage of its boundless fertility by planting crops. The second boast was that the climate was as favourable as the soil. These assertions about empty land could only be made because of some fancy legal footwork by the federal government. Old-time ranchers held vast tracts of the Plains under 20-year leases granted by the federal government. The government in Ottawa opened up vacancies on the range by inserting clauses specifying it could unilaterally take back land on two years notice, simply by declaring it suitable for settlers. This created a complicated legacy of bitter frustration, eventually known as Western Alienation.

As new ranchers and farm homesteaders poured into the West, the cattle industry spread east of its birthplace along the foothills of the Rocky Mountains, into the areas of Eastern Alberta and Western Saskatchewan known as "short-grass country." The vegetation there offered far more sparse grazing than the foothills grasses, which grew tall enough to brush the knees of mounted cowhands.

69

A succession of mild winters and good growing seasons in the late 1880s and '90s allowed promoters to ignore reality. Enthusiasm about the climate knew no bounds. It overtook even the most educated Westerners, like Emily Murphy, the celebrated writer and suffragette who became the first female magistrate in the British Empire. Murphy spread word that the plains were "... a land where sunshine never scorches and yet shade is sweet; where simple pleasures please; where the sky is bright and green fields satisfy forever . . . the whole land is a paradise of blossoms — a very garden of the Lord." And Murphy lived in Edmonton, well beyond reach of all but the strongest Chinooks.

The theory of the reliably gentle climate only stood up among greenhorns. Plains old-timers and the North-West Mounted Police both knew better. A patrol led by NWMP Superintendent James Walsh into short-grass country east of the Cypress Hills in late 1876 spent nine days travelling 100 miles (160 km) on horseback in severe cold, high winds and heavy snow. Only a chance encounter with a handful of buffalo saved the Mounties from having to eat their mounts. Five horses died anyway, on a night so miserable that the patrol's Native guides lost their way. The policemen only survived by staying awake to tramp and hammer themselves to keep from freezing.

Pioneer ranchers never forgot the winter of 1886-87. Many old families still recall it as the worst weather on record. But the title of the worst disaster belongs to the winter of 1906-07, because there were far more people and cattle around for a cold snap to punish.

The great evener arrived in early November of 1906. Veteran plainsmen had spotted warning signs. The horses grew thicker fall coats than normal. Rabbits' fur turned white earlier. Beaver stored extra heavy food caches. In mid-November, the first in a long series of blizzards struck. Temperatures dropped into the -30s Fahrenheit (-35 Celsius) and stayed there until late February, 1907. Although one Chinook blew, it only lasted long enough to create the worst possible conditions for freezing, starving cattle. The warm spell melted the snow just enough to freeze the grass solid when the wind veered back into the north. It locked what little nourishment was available beyond reach of cattle, which "rustle" for feed by digging through snow with their noses. Horses did not fare so badly because they paw snow out of their way with their hooves.

Cattle drifted off their ranges, always to the south, trying to escape biting winds. Ranchers and cowhands tried to control the drift but wound up fighting for their own lives, and could do little to stop the herds. Bearing the brands of many ranches, the herd of starving cattle took more than half an hour to pass the window of a diarist who recorded the grim sight in Fort Macleod.

30° BELOW AT THE OH RANCH

Town officials dragged away 48 carcasses afterwards. Cattle piled up against fences, buildings, stream banks, trees, railway embankments, and in steep-sided plains coulees or canyons. They died in haystacks, by climbing snowdrifts to reach fodder, only to fall inside on top of one another. It took until late April for the snow to melt and reveal the full effects of the evener. Saskatchewan-born author Wallace Stegner, in a family and regional history (*Wolf Willow*, Viking; New York: 1962), conveyed the results in a chapter entitled *Carrion Spring*.

An estimated 50 percent of Western Canada's cattle died. The short-grass ranching boom went bust. Annual livestock sales volumes rose in the fall of 1907 as the hardest-hit ranches folded and owners pulled out, often headed to the U.S. The CPR suspended collecting rentals for ranch leases on its vast land holdings. Ranchers who rented government land and intended to keep operating saved money by letting some of their leases lapse, safe in the knowledge that there would be no competition for grazing space any time soon.

New habits also formed instantly in the growing season of 1907. Virtually all the surviving ranches raised the biggest hay and grain crops they could plant, then stockpiled the harvests as fodder against a repetition of the cold. The community never looked back after learning that winter feedings of hay and grain to cattle did more than save lives in emergencies. They kept animals growing and in good health, accelerating production and improving the livestock's quality, netting ranchers better prices on beef markets, and injecting an element of stability into western livelihoods.

■

■

■

72

THE LAST BEST WEST

AN ANONYMOUS POEM called the Cowboy's Prayer, crafted by unknown idealists around turn-of-the-century campfires, captures how range riders like to see themselves. It has become their code:

O Lord, I've never lived where churches grow;
I've loved creation better as it stood
The day you finished it, so long ago,
And looked upon your work and called it good.
Just let me live my life as I've begun;
And give me work that's open to the sky.
Make me a partner of the wind and sun
And I won't ask for a life that's soft and high.
Make me as big and open as the plains;
As honest as the horse between my knees,
Clean as the wind that blows behind the rains;
Free as the hawk that circles down the breeze.
Just keep an eye on all that's done and said;
Just right me sometime when I turn aside.
And guide me on the long, dim trail ahead
That stretches upward to the Great Divide.

The architect of the greatest memorial to the pioneer and ranching West lived by this code. That architect was Guy Weadick, and his enduring memorial to the Old West is the Calgary Stampede. A larger-than-life figure, Weadick set the tone for the development of Western Canada's imagery and hospitality industry. He built one of Canada's biggest civic events by combining

73

eastern promotional skills and romantic visions with Western Plains history and pastimes. He advertised this trade secret on the cover of his brochures, using the quote, "East is East and West is West, and HERE the twain shall meet. – Kipling revised."

Born in 1885, Weadick grew up in Rochester, N.Y.. At that time, the image of the West as the great lone land of opportunity for adventurous pioneers was at its peak. All young men were urged to go there. He heeded the call at age 17, first travelling with relatives to Manitoba, then heading farther out to the plains on his own. For three years, Weadick roamed as a cowhand and horse wrangler. He worked his way through the Dakotas, Alberta, Montana, Oregon and the southwestern United States to the Mexican border. But it was in Bliss, Oklahoma, home of the Colonel Zack Miller 101 Ranch Wild West Show, that Weadick found his true calling. Miller's organization was a celebrated finishing school for range hands with a yen to perform. Weadick served an apprenticeship there in trick riding and shooting, fancy roping and fairgrounds barking, with household-name stars like Will Rogers, Tom Mix, Goldie St. Clair and Tex McLeod. He travelled with the famous company to Broadway, then on to England, France and Russia. He and his bride, Florence Bensell (on stage, Flores LaDue, World Champion Lady Fancy Roper) first saw Calgary in 1905, in company with a renowned black daredevil steer wrestler named Will Pickett.

Enthusiastic crowds convinced Weadick that he had found a prospective home for a new world capital of rodeo. He went to work on Calgary's business community, starting with livestock agent H.C. McMullen. The CPR horse trader, sniffing an opportunity, introduced Weadick to the movers and shakers in turn-of-the-century Western Canada. By 1912, at age 27, Weadick had rounded up $100,000 from Calgary's entrepreneurial inner circle, the Big Four: George Lane, Pat Burns, A.E. Cross and Archie McLean.

Weadick's show, The Stampede, lived up to its name. Staged in a rainy week following Labour Day of 1912, the event imprinted an indelible memory of success. On opening day alone, the show drew a crowd of 24,000 to the Victoria Park exhibition grounds. This, at a time when the city's population was 61,450. The six-day event recorded 99,447 admissions for $1 apiece, four times the standard ticket price for the more staid agricultural fairs. The opening parade featured NWMP, Natives, stage coaches, Red River carts, artistic floats, rodeo competitors and a thundering herd of 1,000 horses. Estimates of attendance ranged from 60,000 to 75,000, or the entire population of the city plus nearly 14,000 tourists. The event had a wildly exciting finale when a home-grown underdog, Blood Indian Tom Three Persons — granted leave from jail for the occasion — bested a bucking horse named Cyclone which had thrown all other riders.

Legend has it that Weadick's 1912 show did so well with ticket sales that he did not have to touch his backers' cash even after paying expenses, including management fees. Although organizational hitches and World War One postponed repeat performances, a comeback in 1919, titled the Victory Stampede, drew an excellent crowd. Within a year of the 1919 Stampede, Weadick bought the TS spread and went into business as a host for weekend and vacation visitors.

Weadick and the Stampede parted company angrily after the 1932 event. He fought Depression-era managers when they cut rodeo prize money and staff wages in half. The irritated executives fired Weadick, claiming that he showed up drunk at a grandstand ceremony. He won a wrongful dismissal lawsuit, but not reinstatement. Hard feelings on both sides kept him away from the Stampede through the 1930s and '40s. But the southern Alberta social and economic establishment never forgot its debt to his creativity. About 300 ranchers, farmers, business leaders and political figures gave Weadick the only moment ever known to have overwhelmed the great promoter to speechlessness. The community, with ceremonial help from leaders of the Blackfoot Confederacy, presented Weadick and his wife with an engraved watch and cigarette case plus $10,000 cash in August of 1950, as they left to retire to Arizona after selling the TS dude ranch.

Weadick's stroke of genius and his personal popularity, as well as his giant rodeo's success, could be credited to his following the cowboy prayer's prescription for big, open and honest living. From the start, he established the Stampede's formula of aggressive but good-humoured promotion on an international scale. The mammoth fair never pretended to represent the way range riders actually lived and worked every day. The formula started with an admission that the ideal days had come and gone, then based its appeal on strong ingredients of nostalgia and reunion.

Weadick subtitled his original Stampede "The Last Best West." His promotional literature declared, "Not alone the kings and emperors of Rangelands, but citizens of all classes alike have united to make the Stampede a worthy tribute to those grand old men we all delight to honour. But while this is to be a season of joy, a period rich in reminiscences, an occasion of hearty greetings, and renewal of old friendships, there will be just a tinge of sadness as we gaze upon the 'sunset of a dying race.'"

■
■
■

PRINCE OF WALES

THE MAN WHO WOULD NOT BE KING

A QUIET LAY ON THE LAND for decades. Nestled in the Alberta foothills, ranchers followed their annual routines unnoticed, until the summer of 1919. The future King of England, Edward, Prince of Wales, came for a visit and Pekisko Creek and the Canadian West were never the same.

Ranching in the western foothills was well established by the time of the Prince's arrival. During the 1870s, investors had capitalized on the large leases made available to ranches by the Canadian government. Cowboys were riding the range from the Bow River in the north to the Milk River on the American border, gathering herds each spring. But the rangeland in the headwaters of the Highwood River was special. Elsewhere, cold winters drove ice into the hides of even the toughest animals on the prairies. In the foothills, Chinook winds moderated the climate and made for perfect cattle country.

Ranchers were some of the first permanent European residents in the Canadian West. They built a cattle kingdom sandwiched between the buffalo and the settlers, carving out a special place that survives more than a century later. Taking advantage of generous land grants, these cattlemen raised Central Canadian and British capital to build massive herds. With the cash came values and people. Ranchers in the Canadian West differed from their American counterparts. They expected the law and order that the North-West Mounted Police provided. From the old country, they brought polo, tea and high manners, since many were remittance men, sent out from England to make their own way in the far reaches of the Empire.

The British flag flew proudly over the Pekisko Post Office on the Bar U Ranch, south of Longview. From this large western institution, stunning Percherons travelled to shows around North America and Europe, turning heads and winning prizes wherever they went. And so, when the Prince of Wales visited Canada on a Royal Tour in 1919, the Bar U Ranch figured prominently on his itinerary. Across Canada, dignitaries and the common folk flocked to see him. As the symbol of the mother country that so many Canadians fought to save in the Great War, his fresh young face and good looks attracted admiration wherever he went. Hailed by the media as Prince Charming, he was proof of "Britain's imperishable glory."

But Canadians were not the only ones who fell in love in the summer of 1919. Edward also had a good time.

The twenty-five-year-old Prince shot gophers from the train as it chugged between Edmonton and Calgary. At the prestigious Ranchmen's Club in Calgary on September 12, 1919, the Alberta government relaxed strict liquor laws in the Prince's honour. The ranchers and other dignitaries reacted in proper spirit and a provincial judge lead the jubilant crowd in a song with a chorus that went "another little drink won't do us any harm."

However, it was the Prince's visit to the Bar U Ranch that changed the direction of his life. Sixty-three-year-old George Lane, one of the "Big Four" who bankrolled Guy Weadick's first Calgary Stampede in 1912, hosted Edward and entertained him with tales of his adventurous career as a goldminer, Indian scout, teamster and cowboy. Then they shot some ducks.

A.E. Cross, another member of the Big Four and owner of the nearby A7 Ranch, also befriended the Prince. With proud Stoney Natives looking on, the Prince, Cross and Lane watched a fall branding. As the irons scorched their mark on the calves, the smiling royal quipped he was "darn glad he wasn't a calf."

They went for a ride, where the Prince's horsemanship impressed all. No polo or chasing hounds for him. Cowboy life and cattle work enthralled the young man as he watched, learned, and listened. Quietly his heart became attached to this vast new land.

The demanding Royal Tour pulled him away from the Alberta Foothills and his entourage steamed west by train through the spectacular Rockies. A busy schedule tired the less hardy members of his group at official functions in Vancouver and Victoria. During those few days, the Prince decided to buy a piece of the foothills. His infatuation with the ranch country was also a powerful statement of his independence from his overbearing father, much as the Canadian West stands apart from the rest of the country.

On October 7, 1919, the Prince bought a ranch for $130,000 from Frank Bedingfeld and his mother Agnes, homesteaders near the Bar U Ranch since 1886. The deed of sale covered 1,440 acres of freehold land and a half interest in 41,440 acres of leased land on the Pekisko Creek. Also included were 400 horses and 150 cattle.

Years later the Prince said of his EP Ranch in the foothills, "In the midst of that majestic countryside I had suddenly been overwhelmed by an irresistible longing to immerse myself, if only momentarily, in the simple life of the western prairies. There, I was sure, I would find occasional escape from the sometimes too confining, too well ordered island life of Great Britain." He visited when he could, and in 1923 he exchanged royal duties for chores on the ranch. Assuming the life of a gentleman rancher, he fished, rode the range, hunted fowl, rabbits and coyotes, and hosted tea parties for his neighbours.

ROYALTY VISITS THE BAR U RANCH

Most of Edward's visits were short, lasting a few days at most. Ranch managers took care of day-to-day business so that even in the hard times of the 1930s, the EP Ranch stock won prizes in Canada and the United States.

But not all was well with the Prince. Edward became King in early 1936, only to give up the throne in December for "the woman he loved." Prohibited from marrying American divorcee Wallis Simpson, his love affair fascinated the world, and, after Edward abdicated the throne, they were wed in 1937.

Fortune seemed to smile on Edward when the Turner Valley oilfield boomed as the largest in the Empire in the 1940s. As owner of the mineral rights for his ranch, he hoped a well would strike oil on his land. On October 2, 1944, he wrote to his mother, Queen Mary, "It would indeed be a pleasant surprise to wake up finding oneself an oil magnate instead of the impoverished owner of a mere cattle ranch." Although a well on the EP Ranch struck a flow of oil in 1945, water quickly followed.

The ranch diversified further in the 1950s, expanding the horse and cattle operation to include pigs and sheep. Finally, with a sad heart, Edward sold the ranch in 1961. His quiet escape from a busy world in the Alberta Foothills was gone.

Some considered him "the Peter Pan of the Monarchy" for refusing to grow up, for avoiding the responsibilities of his inherited role. But to Westerners, he was a king in cowboy boots, a hero for a new kind of people in a unique frontier, bringing the old and new worlds together.

As a member of the royal family who fell in love with Pekisko Creek, the Man Who Would Not Be King rode into the history of the West as a unique horseman and special rancher.

■

■

■

ENDURANCE

LIFE IN THE SPECIAL AREAS

A ROAD SIGN ON HIGHWAY 9, about 125 miles (200 km) east of Calgary, commemorates John Palliser's 1857 expedition to the North-West Territories, and provides clues for solving the mysteries behind the deserted and weather-beaten barns and ranch houses which jut out of the prairie landscape. A few miles down the highway, another sign announces the boundary to Special Areas — a name which sends shivers through older generations of Western Canadians.

As part of the Royal Geographical Society, and sponsored in part by the British government, Palliser was dispatched to the Canadian West to evaluate the land and its suitability for settlement. For two years Palliser criss-crossed the prairies as far west as the Rocky Mountains. He was assisted by botanist Eugene Bourgeau and Dr. James Hector, a geologist and naturalist. Palliser's report was definitive. In his opinion, the southwestern prairies were simply an extension of the northern United States desert. This area was not suitable for homesteaders.

But Canada had an agenda to settle the West. With literature from the government and the railways flooding Europe, new settlers were being lured to the Canadian West. In 1901 there were a mere 75 people residing in an area which extends from Suffield in the south, north to Consort and west from the Saskatchewan border to Hanna. By 1918, 26,000 people and 27,000 horses had come to homestead in what would later be called Special Areas. They had crossed the Atlantic Ocean and ridden Canada's new national railway to take advantage of the offer of 160 acres of free land in the Eden of the West. If they stayed for three years, they could also have another "pre-emption" of 160 acres.

Palliser's warnings had been forgotten.

With this massive surge of new homesteaders, and a coming of age in World War One, Canada had become a nation famous for wheat. By 1928, Canada accounted for half of the world's wheat exports.

But things were not as rosy in the Special Areas. Doomed to a 20 year cycle — ten years of wet weather and reasonable crops followed by ten years of dry — this vast area of the new province of Alberta was constantly plagued by drought. The area had long-term average annual rainfalls of only 12 inches, and an 80 percent chance that only eight inches of precipitation would fall.

The sandy soil, of poor quality at best, would blow away in the vicious westerly winds which howled almost constantly. Today, regulators suggest average stocking rates should not exceed one cow and calf for every 48 acres, less than four cows for each historic homestead.

By the mid-1920s, the weather cycle had switched over to dry and conditions worsened rapidly. In 1926, a Royal Commission was struck to study the disaster unfolding in southeastern Alberta. Three out of four homesteading attempts had failed and the region's inhabitants were desperate.

The next 15 years saw conditions deteriorate further as the Great Depression and almost complete drought descended on the land like a funeral shroud. The railways and the provincial and federal governments initiated a program to help farmers who were completely ruined. They offered free rail passes to leave the Special Areas. Over 1,300 families took the free passes and, in 2,200 rail cars, they shipped their lives from the southern prairies. While their owners packed up and left, horses and other stock were turned loose and abandoned.

By 1948, the Crown had taken back three million acres from farmers who couldn't pay their taxes. Thirty-seven municipal districts were completely bankrupt. In total, there were five million acres (21,000 km²) which would be designated as Special Areas. By 1948, the population had dropped to 6,000 (its current level).

Bankrupt, but driven to make their way in Canada, many homesteaders went north and west to Peace River and Eckville and tried again, many with success. But there were a few who continued in the Special Areas.

The Pugh clan has survived in the Special Areas for four generations. Joseph and Adelia, the English originals, were born in 1874 and emigrated from Manchester. The couple rose to the lures cast for immigrants by the Canadian government and Canadian Pacific Railway. They reached the plains at Dorothy, beside the Red Deer River downstream from Drumheller, in 1911. Hard labour started immediately. The Pughs packed in a box-car load of lumber, six horses, a cow, chickens and household goods. It was 30 miles (47 km) from the nearest station on the Canadian Pacific Railway, at Bassano. After seven years of struggling to support seven children on stony ground watered by as little as two inches (5 cm) of rain per year, Adelia took a job as postmistress in Dorothy in 1918. Rheumatism and dry years finally drove Joseph off the land and into town in 1931. Eldest son Fred continued the struggle, first, on the original Pugh homestead, and then again on a new one nearby. But the hard climate, poor soil, grasshoppers, long distances to markets and perennially weak commodity prices turned the homesteaders' dream upside down. Instead of living off the

ABANDONED FRIEND

land, Fred and Vera Pugh wound up working almost every waking moment to support their homestead as well as their five children. The couple thanked coal mining at Drumheller and East Coulee for creating local markets. They bought pigs and calves, butchered them and peddled the pork and veal. They dealt in home-made butter, buns and doughnuts. This second generation of plains Pughs eventually faced up to hard realities by leaving the land for a town store and post office. By the 1930s, Calgary and its Stampede were big enough to spell real possibilities of income. Fred Pugh entered a chuckwagon in the Calgary races during 1933 and 1934 and placed well.

Fred's eldest son Ed went to work ranching on horseback. After serving in the army during the Second World War at camps in Quebec and Ontario, where he met wife Edna, he went back to work on ranches in the Dorothy district. He rose quickly to foreman, a job that even after the 1930s Great Depression ended still paid just $70 a month.

In 1944, he began his long association with the Calgary Stampede as a wrangler, trailing rodeo stock from horse ranching country around Dorothy west to the city. The long trail drives lasted until 1964. The fair's Calgary Stampede Ranch switched to highway trucks and trailers in 1965, but revived the old days by commissioning Ed to lead an old-fashioned 140-mile (225 km) trail drive into the 75th-anniversary rodeo in 1987.

The effort to make western land pay continues. Ed's daughter Joan, as a Prairie Farm Rehabilitation Administration hand and business woman, leads a movement for change in the Special Areas. The new strategy puts away ploughs and restores the land to its original condition by replanting the short, hard native grasses which the pioneers called prairie wool. "There's not much of it, but what there is, is good," Joan says. While a tractor sits in a garage, she and partner Ed Campion run about 500 cattle with a handful of horses quartered in a barn built in 1917. They reclaimed the barn from the crop of abandoned buildings left by failed farms.

The Special Areas claimed many victims, but the Pughs, with dedication and creativity, managed to find a way to carve out a living in one of the toughest areas in the province of Alberta.

■ ■ ■

BERT SHEPPARD
A LEGEND IN CATTLE COUNTRY

ARM SWINGING AN IMAGINARY QUIRT, legs jamming out sideways, Bert Sheppard was riding a bronc at age 94. Never mind that the saddle was perched precariously on a stand in his basement. In his mind's eye, he was 24 again. Wiry, lean, determined to stay with any mount, no matter how rank, Bert was showing off the style that made him a legend.

Joe Clark once called Bert a "national institution." Coming from a man who grew up in High River, Alberta, and became Prime Minister of Canada, the compliment sits well on the shoulders of the small cowboy.

When Bert came into the world on February 26, 1901, his family owned the Cottonwood Ranch near High River. Only four Sheppard children survived the brutal conditions of the turn of the century. Bert, youngest and smallest, remembers a "good mother, stern father," and a busy home. Listening to stories on his mother's knee, Bert fell in love with cowboy life. But his parents made it clear that before Bert could pursue any cowboy dreams, he was expected to get an education. And so he did, in a brick school house in High River.

Shortly after celebrating his twenty-first birthday, Bert found himself working at the Bar U Ranch. For several summers, Bert broke horses, rode herd, worked brandings, and learned the cowboy life well. Even after leaving the Bar U, he continued to break horses for the ranch. He would ride up from his parents' ranch on the Highwood River each Sunday and collect six wild broncs. The next weekend, he would ride back with them all broken. As a young man learning the ropes, Bert took most everything the oldtimers said to heart. "The old way of doing things was to manoeuvre the herd in such a way that the cattle were happy to be doing what you wanted them to do," says Bert.

Keeping cattle happy was relatively easy compared to staying afloat financially. Cattle prices fell apart in 1920 and stayed low until 1927, only to plummet again in the 1930s. A severe drought plagued the Highwood valley during the Depression. In the hot summer of 1936, a forest fire nearly wiped out every living thing in the foothills. In spite of the tough times, Bert managed to make good. After his father's death in 1934, he took over the Riverbend Ranch near Longview. Along with Joe and John Bews and Raymond Patterson, he bought the famous OH Ranch in 1939. By 1950, he was managing the famous OH Ranch, which dates back to 1883, and in 1961 he became part owner. Over the decades, Bert taught dozens of cowboys, chirping hints into their ears day after day. Retirement came in 1963.

Along the way, Bert's sharp eye recognized the artistic talents of a handful of budding artists, and he encouraged them by giving them work on the ranch. He also bought their art. The first artist, Bert Smith, arrived at the TL on Christmas Day, 1950, for a three-day visit. Three years of cowboyin' later, the commercially trained artist had a new appreciation for life on the range. His photos and paintings truly captured ranch life along the Highwood River. Others followed in his boots, including Mac Mackenzie, Rich Roenisch, Gaile Gallup, Gary Foster, Steve Hoar and Bob Spaith.

When the time came to capture Bert's own likeness on canvas, he wanted to be portrayed riding a bronc. Bert says modern rodeo riders use different saddles and ride in a style that gives a great show. They are expected "to act like a cross between a monkey and a wildcat for ten seconds and give the horse all they've got in that time." As skilled as today's rodeo champions are, breaking horses for a living 70 years ago was a different game altogether.

Even though he wanted to be portrayed as a bronc rider, Bert was certainly no rodeo cowboy. Indeed, he says he performed mostly for an audience of coyotes. But off and on, he tamed horses for about 17 years. "Horse breaking consists of encouraging the horse to do the right things and discouraging him from doing the wrong," he says simply.

Breaking horses was brutal work and called for the right equipment. In the 1920s, this bronco twister used a special saddle. Bert's high-horned, centre-fire outfit cost him $27 and was built by W.D. Horner of Heppner, Oregon. It featured a narrow fork, high and sloped forward. He says the high horn was easy to grab as the cowboy slid into the saddle in the split second before the horse exploded. The sloping cantle helped the rider stay in the middle of the saddle. A sparse supply of leather in the seat ensured close contact with the horse.

All these features placed the rider over the balance point of the horse, giving him a chance to stay with the bucking mount 'til it gave up the fight. Bert's saddle also included tapaderos, heavy covered stirrups that helped the rider stay with the mount. Taps were a great help, but if you didn't get your foot into the far stirrup fast enough, it could fly up and knock you senseless. A quirt, held with the first two fingers of the right hand, came into action on the flanks of the horse on its way down from the first leap, before it contacted the ground.

In a contest between a small, wiry cowboy and a large, out-of-control horse, the cowboy needed every advantage a

EARNIN' HIS BREAD AND BUTTER

saddlemaker could provide. The rest was up to him. Strong legs held Bert in the saddle. With his left elbow at his side, he let horses have "all the head they wanted" and went for the ride. Boots firmly planted in the taps, he turned his toes up as the horse vaulted skyward, then threw the taps out sideways to help break the jar of the fall. Even still, when the second foot hit, "it just about crumpled you."

When things went well, it was a great way to make a living. But there were bad days too, like when the horse went down. One bounced Bert's head on the ground so hard that he heard nothing at dinner. Hours later, his hearing started coming back. In total, Bert rode hundreds of bucking mounts, once going for a decade without being thrown. Finally, however, his insides "got churned" and he started spitting blood. In his day, that was a powerful hint to take up a new line of work.

Over the years, Bert passed on the knowledge of many great cattlemen of the Canadian West. Bert learned from them all, but in fact, few could equal Bert's roping skill. At one branding, he heeled three calves a minute, probably the fastest time on record. Decades later, Bert said it took a bit of imagination to rope that fast and "make it look easy."

As a witness to floods and droughts, killer blizzards and choking forest fires, Bert Sheppard has lived his whole life along the banks of the Highwood River. "Be Prepared for Anything" is the motto that guides the ranchers in this valley. As cowboy, bronc rider, cattleman and philanthropist, Bert Sheppard is a living legend.

■
■
■

HERMAN LINDER

A COWBOY'S COWBOY

CANADIAN COWBOYS and rodeo livestock sent British sports fans into rhapsodies when some of the best from the west went overseas for the first time in 1934. The wild spectacle of dare devil cowboys spurring like madmen on board bucking broncos made a striking first impression on the English crowd. Among the cowboys in the arena that year was Herman Linder.

Known as the rodeo cowboy's cowboy, Linder was one of the top cowboys in the history of rodeo. He was also a spokesman for the rights of cowboys and a producer of some of the biggest rodeos in Canada. But what stands out the most when one looks at the life and legend of Linder is his reputation as a gentleman and an icon of integrity and high ideals. Straightforward and honest, he has a great respect and concern for his peers and, even with his fame, has remained a gentleman, humble and gracious. In short, Linder is the consummate cowboy.

The rodeo troop which took Linder to Britain in 1934 was from Austin, Texas. A spiritual descendant of Buffalo Bill Cody's Wild West Show, it introduced Canadians to the world, including Pete Knight, hero of the bucking horse. An English newspaper sports writer expressed the admiration of enthusiastic crowds after seeing a performance, writing, "If you get a man as hard as nails, as brave as a lion, as active as a cat and as lithe as a serpent, then you have a cowboy."

Herman Linder was all of these things and more. As the biggest winner of them all, Linder personified the breed, equal parts plainsman, performer and professional. He set the standard in the arenas during ten years as a professional competitor, from 1929 to 1939. He won 22 championships at the Calgary Stampede, including the Canadian All-Round Rodeo Championship seven times, and the North American All-Round trophy five times. Not only did he win in his specialty, saddle broncs, but also in calf roping and in bareback, bull and wild steer riding.

Linder always maintained that champions are born, not made, because no amount of schooling can give rodeo performers the raw material they need both to win and have a decent life expectancy — quick reflexes and sharp wits. With a Swiss father who was an acrobat, Herman had the right genes. Rather than settle for the meagre prospects available to a retired circus performer in his native Alps, Linder's father emigrated to become a cheese maker in Wisconsin and Illinois.

Born in Illinois in 1907, Herman Linder was 11 years old when his family bought a farming and cattle spread in southwestern Alberta, near Cardston. Young Herman, inspired by the era's abundant adventure tales about the pioneer west, fell in love with the Canadian version as soon as the family moved out to its new home on the range. He recalled the 1918 street sounds of Cardston as horses' hooves and jingling tack. He vowed to become a cowboy just like the ones he saw decked out in their best spur-jangling and tall-hatted town gear.

Linder graduated from farmyard rough-housing to rodeo arenas at age 14. He made his first appearance at Cardston in 1921. By 1929, he had risen from the small-town rodeo circuit to be a Calgary Stampede star, winning the saddle and bareback bronc prizes his first time out at the big show. For the next decade, he bucked and roped around the globe as a top performer before packed grandstands, from the Chicago World's Fair to Australia. He plowed his earnings into the family spread.

Things did not just happen often to this cowboy — they occurred "as regularly as a cow bloats on fresh alfalfa." After his first taste of the fun, glory and cash to be had on the circuit, there was no keeping Linder down on the farm during rodeo seasons, June through November. "One of my greatest thrills was that Saturday night when they awarded the prizes at the grandstand," said Linder. "There I was, standing with a gold watch in each hand, with the fireworks exploding all around me. The thought that I still had $800 cash money to collect over at the office was almost too much for me. That $800 was more money than I had ever hoped to see in my life all at one time."

Linder regularly won $5,000 to $8,000 a year, a king's ransom during the '30s Great Depression. He also had good reason to emerge as a labour leader on an American branch of the professional circuit. Rodeo was a hard and precarious living, with a strong element of exploitation by aggressive promoters. Except for the modest wages paid by international travelling shows to cowboys to look after the livestock, rodeo riders had to rely on their winnings. An injured man only got sympathy.

Frustration burst into the open in 1936 when Linder led a group called the "Cowboy Turtles," a name intended to send a message that even if cowboys start slowly, they always reach their destination. They took on a Boston promoter named W.T. Johnson by going on strike. Johnson hired stable hands to replace the 61 strikers. But, with help from the crowd at the Boston Gardens, which jeered the stable hands, Linder won a 60-percent increase in the Boston rodeo's prize money and refunds of cowboys' entry fees.

Linder explained, "This trouble had been building up for many years. The cowboy was just considered incidental to the

WINNING IT ALL

show. He had to travel great distances at his own expense, in the hopes of winning some prize money. And he had to put up an entry fee just to get into the contest. At some shows, the prize money wasn't much more than the combined entry fees. In other words, the cowboys were risking their necks to win back their own money. You can get better odds than that in any poker game."

Following his retirement from competition in 1939, Linder moved into event management. In this executive role, he again became a champion — this time, of rodeo's right to exist at all. The sport has always run afoul of professed animal lovers. In Vancouver in 1949, the local SPCA and a hostile news media hounded the police into laying cruelty charges against Linder as manager of a rodeo for a city Rotary Club. It took a year-long fight, all the way to the Supreme Court of British Columbia, for Linder to win a not-guilty verdict following judicial scrutiny of his rodeo. It was another decade before rodeo was attempted again in Vancouver. But the clean bill of health that case established for the sport stood everywhere else.

Canadian to the core, Linder played down the violent side of the cowboy image fostered by the original wild-west shows and dime novels, and continued by the movies. "I never carried a gun in my life. For one thing, it's against the law. And it would sure be dangerous, because all the other cowboys would die laughing if they saw you walking around toting one."

■

■

■

CASEY TIBBS

CHAMPION BRONC RIDER

THE WALL-EYED BRONC snorts and gives a little buck — just a taste of what is to come later. The cowboy, non-plussed by the horse's gesture, continues to work on cinching up his custom-made buckin' saddle. High cantle, big swells and a low seat to keep him close to the bronc, he finishes his task and swings his leg over the top rail of the chute. With the horse-hair shank in his left hand, he settles deep into the saddle, leans back and puts his spurs over the shoulders of the vibrating horse. Casey Tibbs nods his head, the gate swings open and the crowd is in for another show.

If past statistics are any guide, Tibbs will ride this bronc out — he was only bucked off six times in 280 rides in 1951. Duded up in a trademark lavender shirt and kerchief, this lean, wiry cowboy was a legend by the time he was 22 years old, hailed as one of the greatest saddle and bareback bronc riders ever to enter an arena.

Born March 5, 1929 in a log house on a homestead on the Cheyenne River in South Dakota, Casey was the youngest of ten children. His parents told his siblings a coyote brought him while they were away at school. From the start, Casey was different. Independent and possessed with fierce determination, he attacked life. Casey wouldn't just ride the 10 miles (16 km) to school each day, he'd work that old mare out, getting her to buck and constantly honing his horsemanship.

By age 14, Casey had run away from home to enter his first rodeo. "I figured that rodeoing would be a lot easier than ranch work," he said. Eight years later, Tibbs would grace the cover of *Life Magazine*, acknowledged as the best in the business. Over the course of his career, Tibbs made more money than most cowboys ever dream of, winning $21,000 in 1949, his rookie year. That year, he was also World Saddle Bronc Champion. He won it every year from 1951 to 1954, taking the honour again in 1959. For winning the most points and contest money, Tibbs also received the World All-Around Championship in 1951 and 1955.

Life Magazine's October 1951 edition, with Casey Tibbs splashed over the cover, sold over five million copies. For twenty cents, any rodeo fan could buy the magazine and read "Champ Rider: Casey Tibbs has a rip-roaring time on the broncs and off." At age 22, he became the first man ever to win the bareback and saddle bronc championships in the same year. Madison Square Gardens was his as the crowds cheered the young man from the banks of the Cheyenne.

Never shy, Casey loved to talk about his work of riding broncs. "You jus' fall into the rhythm and it's like dancing with a girl," he said. But if the bronc "starts mixing up his tricks, you gotta know your business. If you don't, you'll either pop your gizzard or eat dirt." At six feet tall, and weighing only 150 pounds, Tibbs had an ideal body for riding broncs. Blessed with balance and rhythm which kept him glued on during most rides, Tibbs took his physical advantages for granted. "I don't have to last 15 rounds like a boxer," he said. "I am on and off a bronc before I can take a deep breath." Tibbs' spectacular spurring made him a crowd favourite wherever he went. With his purple shirts and loud kerchiefs, Tibbs created a rodeo cowboy persona that he wore like a badge.

Casey Tibbs was more than just a great buckin' horse rider. He was a sex symbol for a generation of young rodeo fans. Described as "the kind of cowboy that the gals sure do take to," women worshiped him. Casey acknowledged ladies were one of his vices. "Pretty women are my weakness. A fella jus' can't help loving 'em all," he said. But dice, booze, the occasional brawl and driving his purple Cadillac at outrageous speeds were also passions for Tibbs. He boasted of his skills as a pugilist — "A rodeo cowboy's got a lot of determination and in a street fight, he makes up for short wind that way." He was known for carrying a pair of green dice with him wherever he went. In one stay in Nevada, he lost $11,000 at craps and poker, a king's ransom in the early 50s. But Tibbs could afford it. The hours in the saddle were short and the pay cheques big.

True to his image, Tibbs lived the life of a wild man, driving his Caddy at 95 miles an hour (150 km/h) between rodeos in Calgary, Cheyenne and New York. Tibbs was working both sides of the border, and taking big pay cheques away. He often competed at the Calgary Stampede in the 1950s, where half a million people attended the "Greatest Outdoor Show On Earth." When he rode, 25,000 pairs of eyes watched their hero. But, this spectacular life was hard on Tibbs' body. During his career, he broke thirty bones, including ribs and his left ankle as well as suffering some knee damage. Fearless on horseback, he once speculated that if he was ever killed, it would "probably be in my Cadillac."

Over time, Tibbs settled somewhat. He saved some cash and bought a Hereford cattle ranch with his brother in South Dakota. He tried to retire from rodeo in 1960, but the broncs kept him coming back a few times each year until the late '60s. Even then, he never quit living the high life. He turned his charm and good looks to other vistas. He went to Hollywood and pursued a career on the big screen. As an actor, he and his horse, Midnight, became known to millions. He also produced westerns, including a documentary called *Born to Buck*.

The 49th parallel has never meant much to Westerners. Long before North American Free Trade arrived, cattle and

AN AMERICAN LEGEND

cowboys routinely crossed the border between Canada and the United States, driving herds of cattle and finding work on whatever ranch was hiring. That tradition continues with rodeo cowboys. Casey Tibbs was a charismatic hero whose fame and talents spanned the entire continent. Decked out in loud purple colours, Tibbs' long spurring strokes and exceptional style made him a legend and a crowd-pleaser wherever he went. His name is etched forever in record books on both sides of the border.

■

■

■

PLAINS CHARIOTS

CHUCKWAGON RACES TOP RODEO DRAMA

EXCITEMENT BUILDS IN THE CROWD as they watch four wagons make their way to the infield, each pulled by four hot-blooded Thoroughbreds and accompanied by four "outriders," also mounted on fast racehorses. The drivers jockey their 1,300 pound (577 kg) wagons into position near the starting barrels. The outriders dismount and take their spots. One, with the reins of his horse in his teeth, helps keep the lead team settled and positioned to cut the first corner of the figure-eight. His compatriots move to the back of the wagon. One will toss a 35-pound (15 kg) stove into the wagon while the other two will toss the two tent poles which hold a tarp over the stove.

The crowd shifts to the edge of their seats. The only sound is the snorting of 32 horses and the jingle of tack as the massive animals shuffle and paw in anticipation. Seemingly without warning, the klaxon sounds.

"Annnd they'rrrre offffff!" drawls the announcer. With a slap of the reins, the driver spurs his team into action, cutting a right-hand turn around the first barrel. The outriders, having completed their duties, scramble to get out of the way and mount their eager steeds, knowing they have to be within 120 feet of their wagon at the finish line. The wagons, running four abreast, wheel to wheel, skid through the final left-hand turn onto the race track. Mud flies, drivers shout and outriders scramble to catch up. It's a chuckwagon race.

The true origins of wagon racing are hard to track. Some say the sport originated in spontaneous races during cattle drives before fences criss-crossed the Canadian West. Having hot grub ready at the end of the day was a point of pride among the men who drove the original range wagons. They would race the 2,000 pound (900 kg) wagons to that night's camp and see who could get coffee ready first. Other versions say they raced to saloons at the end of cattle drives, with rival outfits betting drinks on the outcome. Still others say the sport is rooted in the rivalries between stagecoach companies, and to land rushes on the American frontier, where land authorities had homesteaders line up for races to the best land.

The "chucks" became the Calgary Stampede's most popular event from their first race in 1923. It worked because there was more than a grain of truth in the circus-style hyperbole used by Calgary Stampede founder Guy Weadick.

"Primitive, rattling, lumbering, range-scarred mess wagons," said Weadick's promotional literature. "Their daring drivers on the swaying seats, handling the ribbons on the fastest four-horse team their ranch can produce. Old-timers who know no fear, and daredevil young-uns desperately pitting their skill in racing rivalries. They break camp, load their wagons, cut a figure-eight and run . . . the sensation of any race course. The mad glories of the chariot races of the Roman Coliseum eclipsed by the rangemen of the west."

Originally, racers loaded up genuine iron stoves and heats ended only after they unpacked and lighted the stoves at the finish line. Victory went to the first team to show a puff of smoke. However, issues of safety and care for the horses have resulted in many changes to the sport. Today's racing wagon is a cut down version of the original. The stove rack has been moved to help prevent injury, and iron stoves have been replaced with rubber imitations. Barrels used to mark the figure-eight are also made of rubber so they will collapse if hit by a wagon. Care for the horses has also improved, starting with a ban against whips which has evolved into strict regulation, including SPCA supervision, veterinary inspections and drug testing.

Despite the changes, the event remains a contest of wood, leather, iron, horseflesh and hard men. There would be no wagon races, and only pile-ups at great expense to life, limb and gear, if everyone did not keep out of each other's way — if only by inches. When the announcer howls, "they are wheel to wheel down the back stretch," he is more precise than most fans realize.

Wagon racers take pride in being men of action, using no more words than are strictly necessary. Sprains and broken bones are rarely mentioned, much less complained about. A visitor to the barns behind the rodeo grounds is expected to be observant enough to notice a bandaged wrist and swollen thumb, and be careful with that handshake. But eloquence can come to even the strongest and most silent when a friend who has lived by the code dies by it.

Robert Magee's *Quick Start* depicts the mass rush onto the track after a close start. The driver on the far left is George Normand, a six-time world-champion driver dubbed the Bonnyville Bullet, a reference to his northeast Alberta home town and his fierce nature as a competitor. Normand died in a quick start at age 38 in Ponoka, where the annual rodeo serves as a warmup for Calgary's Stampede each July. A rubber barrel in the infield failed to collapse quickly enough when his wagon hit it. The jolt pitched Normand out of his seat, and a wheel dealt a fatal blow to his head as he hit the track. It was the eighth fatality in the 72-year history of organized chuckwagon racing.

Normand is still celebrated as a racer who had the good sense to be in control, both on the track and off. He had a business

QUICK START

in raising, training and trading outrider and wagon horses, which helped him become one of a very few full-time professionals in this rodeo specialty, doing well enough to support his wife and two children. In lamenting the death of Normand as the loss of an ideal type, peers made known the qualities their communities aspire to attain. Courage ranks high, beside independence, self-control and technical mastery.

"We can't let fear do anything to our sport," said Don Chapin, a veteran of more than two decades in chuckwagon drivers' seats, who raced at Ponoka with a broken heel. "We'd all be quitting. George wouldn't have wanted that. I saw him take other tumbles. He didn't cry about it. Next day, he was up and at it again." Ward Willard, another wagon racing mainstay and former champion, described Normand as the chuckwagon racer's racer because "he did not play games out there. He ran fair and still won. He won all his races fair."

The mourning racers allowed a rare glimpse into the impulse which keeps them on the track, often in celebrated father-son driver dynasties. Their surnames, Cosgrave, Dorchester and Glass, have become household words as rodeo royalty in the West. How can they keep going out for a regional sport after it proves it can kill even its best?

"It's a beautiful sport," Chapin insists. "Not everybody can jump on a wagon, grab four lines, have fun, enjoy it and be competitive." Willard, the 1990s head of a champion family stretching back into the early 1950s, says, "you're drawn to it like a moth to a flame. There's an element of danger in it, sure. It's part of the territory. You have to accept it. It's a good sport. I have more fear on the Deerfoot Trail (freeway) through Calgary."

■

■

■

TOMMY BEWS

MAKING OF A LEGEND

THERE IS SOMETHING EXTRA to Tommy Bews. There is something in the very fibre of this Alberta cowboy, a driven single-mindedness, something in his genetic code that makes Tom Bews what he is — one of the finest horsemen and greatest rodeo cowboys ever to buck it out in an arena. But Tom Bews is more than just a successful cowboy. He is also a teacher and mentor to a whole new generation.

Born in High River in 1944, Tom knew as soon as he could walk that he wanted to be a cowboy. Growing up on the family's historic Y-Cross Ranch west of Longview, Tom's apprenticeship started immediately under the watchful eye and skilful hands of his father Joe. Throughout his youth, Tom was riding the range, breaking colts and working mother cows on the tough ridges of the Y-Cross. In those days, Tom was completely single-minded about his future. Regular school just got in the way of more important learning. "Hell, I had bigger and better things to do. I wanted to rope and ride buckin' horses," chuckles Tom. By age 15, after various attempts by his parents and teachers to forestall the inevitable, Tom's headmaster in Regina sent him home. For Tom, the timing couldn't have been better. He would make it back in time for the 1960 Little Britches Rodeo in Calgary.

But even at home, he wasn't always happy. He would regularly migrate between the Y-Cross and the neighbouring OH Ranch, where manager Bert Sheppard would take him in and put him to work for a couple of weeks. "I'd get upset and I'd ride down and get with Bert," recalls Tom. When he'd had enough of Bert and the OH, he'd ride back over Whiskey Ridge, home to the Y-Cross.

It was a constant quest, learning as much as he could about horses and how to handle them. With his family, Tom showed horses throughout the 1950s and 60s, regularly winning classes for western pleasure, western riding and reining at such prestigious events as the Calgary International Horse Show. But he wanted to learn more. Tom had already "started lots of broncy colts" and worked to produce some fine ranch and show horses, but he wanted to master another type of horsemanship. "I wanted to learn the skills of rodeo arena horses," he says. So, in the fall of 1961, Tom's father arranged for Tom to work in Edmonton with Billy Collins, a former Canadian calf roping champion and the king of reining, cutting and showing horses. Tom was still single-minded.

By 1962, Tom had begun his professional rodeo career riding saddle broncs in both the pro and novice events as well as bull dogging and calf roping. He also worked as a pick-up man for rodeo stock legends Harry Vold and Reg Kesler. In 1964, Tom got his pro card and gave up novice saddle bronc. That year he won the Professional Rodeo Cowboy Association's Rookie Bronc Rider of the World. Two years later, Tom won his first Canadian All-Around Championship, finishing in the top ten in all three of his disciplines. He followed that up in 1967 by winning the North American and Canadian All-Around Championships at the Calgary Stampede. When he retired from rodeo in 1984, Tom had won the Canadian All-Around Championship five times, the first cowboy ever to achieve this mark.

At the Medicine Hat Rodeo in 1963, he met Rosemarie Linder, the daughter of famous bronc rider Herman Linder. In August of 1965 they were wed. Like Tom, Rosemarie has the same drive and single-mindedness. Together, they were virtually unstoppable.

Getting married didn't even cause a pause in Tom's increasingly successful rodeo career. Rosemarie joined him on the road and by 1966, the first of four sons was born. TJ was followed by Guy, Dusty and Peter. All four young men have the same special qualities of their father. They are accomplished cowboys and horsemen in their own right, competing in rodeos, breaking and training horses, and working as stunt men and wranglers on movie sets throughout North America.

Despite incredible success in the rodeo arena, Tom knew he still had more to learn. The winters of 1967 and 1968, Tom went to Texas to learn from Neil Love, a guru in the world of training calf roping and bull dogging horses. "I spent many hours in the pens trying to better my timed events," recalls Tom. "I started a lot of bull doggin' horses. Neil wanted a horse to bring me in and then break out left, instead of going straight through." At five feet, ten inches and weighing in at 170 pounds, Tom was at least 30 pounds lighter than most of his competitors in the bull dogging events. But his prowess and skill in training horses gave him an edge over his opponents and in 1971, he won the Canadian Steer Wrestling and Saddle Bronc Championships as well as the Canadian All-Around title.

It was that ability to train bull dogging horses which helped Tom and Rosemarie feed their growing family in the early years. "When I got one working right," Tom says of his steer wrestling mounts, "someone would offer me money, and I'd let him go. That was a way of making the money work."

By 1970, Tom and Rosemarie had a big enough bankroll to purchase a place of their own, the historic South Fork Trading

102

WRANGLIN' UP THE HORSES

Post on the Stimson Creek, south of Longview. For four years, Rosemarie managed and ran the store, while Tom rodeoed and trained horses. By 1972, Tom was hosting and teaching rodeo schools on their Pekisko property, already embarking on the next phase of his career.

Three years later, Tom started moonlighting in the movie business. He worked on *Mustang Country* with Joel McCrae and coached Paul Newman on his horsemanship for the film *Buffalo Bill and the Indians*. Tom's association with the movie business has continued on and off for the past 20 years, with work on movies like *Gunsmoke*, the Japanese epic *Heaven and Earth*, where Tom was the stock coordinator for 750 horses, and Academy Award winning *Unforgiven* with Clint Eastwood. He was also stock coordinator for the weekly television series *Lonesome Dove*.

In 1980, Rosemarie, Tom and their family moved to their current home, The Big Loop Cattle Company on the north bank of the Highwood River west of Longview. Together they have built a beautiful log home and a covered arena where Tom can continue his work breaking and training horses for rodeo work, team roping and ranch work. Tom is cattle ranching and still hosting rodeo schools, teaching team roping clinics, and working in the film business. "Horses and the cattle business are my life," he says simply. "I'm going to keep my boots on and keep riding 'til I'm six feet under." Single-mindedness, a passion for excellence and good old-fashioned hard work have made Tommy Bews a living legend.

■

■

■

104

BRANDINGS

PICKING THE CREW

COWBOYS ARE REMARKABLE for their respect of tradition. Each day, as they saddle up and ride out, they do everything in much the same way their great-grandfathers did. Horsemanship, good "cow sense," pride in the way they handle a rope and the annual spring branding have endured all of the changes to the ranching industry.

To the outside observer, a branding will look chaotic. Bellowing mother cows, bawling calves, horses, ropes, red-hot irons and the smell of burning hide pervade and overwhelm almost every sense. After a while, the scene seems to change. There is order and direction in that mayhem. Everyone has a job to do, and despite the crazy look to it all, everybody seems intent on their task.

The branding starts with a "gather." Neighbours meet at the barns at daybreak, saddled and ready to ride. Under the direction of the "cow boss," the cowboys ride out and sweep the entire pasture, collecting every animal into one large herd. Cattle are driven to the "branding trap," usually a temporary corral close to the cattle. After the entire herd is collected, the mother cows are "cut off" the calves. But the cow boss always leaves a few old mother cows in the pen to keep the calves a little more settled. Then, the real work of branding begins.

There is a lot of tradition, a lot of pride and a lot of common sense in organizing the branding crew. Age, experience and skill all play a role in how the cow boss delegates jobs.

First he picks his "heelers." These cowboys need to have a "hot hand," able to consistently rope calves by both back legs. "One hocking," or roping only one of the back legs, is frowned upon and makes extra work for the "rasslers." Heelers also have to "dally" right, wrapping the rope around the horn of the saddle, leaving the right distance between horse and calf. Too close or too long also means extra work for the rasslers. Heelers need steady horses who won't balk at the stench, the noise or the fire used to heat the irons. These horses must be quiet, consistent mounts who will carefully and quietly pick their way through bunched-up, frightened calves.

Heelers know they are the stars of the branding. How quickly they rope and how efficiently they move will decide how well the branding goes. For heelers, branding is a chance to show their skills with a rope. They aren't showing off, they're just proving their prowess, a subtle, but important difference.

The lowest rung of the branding crew ladder is the rassler. Working in pairs, these men are responsible for immobilizing the calf while "iron men," "cutters," "de-horners," and "shooters" do their work. Rassling calves is a messy, dirty and, occasionally, dangerous job. These men are in the dirt and dung with their noses inches away from the smoke of the irons. For these reasons, the cow boss selects the greenhorns, the youngest, least experienced men of the crew.

But, like heelers, rasslers also determine how successful a branding will be. If they are efficient and consistent, it makes the whole day go a little easier.

An observer watching rasslers will soon conclude it's a job which takes a great deal of strength and agility. While agility is necessary, proper technique and timing means the job doesn't require great strength. Children as young as ten years old can rassle, if they use the right techniques.

Rasslers take up positions on opposite sides of the rope as the heeler drags the calf close to the branding fire. One man grabs the rope and the other takes the tail of the calf. While one works the rope in a rowing motion, the other tugs the tail of the calf down. With proper timing, very little effort is required to tip the calf on its side. As soon as the calf is tipped, the tail man moves to the front of the calf, puts his knee over the calf's neck and curls the top front leg to immobilize the front of the calf. When he has control of the front, the other rassler sets to immobilize the hindquarters. Assuming a sitting position, he pushes the bottom back leg of the calf forward using his high-heeled cowboy boot. The upper back leg is stretched back. The hindquarters rassler removes the rope and the heeler goes back for another.

As well as immobilizing the calf, rasslers are responsible for telling the de-horner which tools he needs and for ensuring all of the tasks are completed on each calf.

The cow boss also selects iron men, cutters, de-horners and shooters based on experience, age and skill. Iron men will be the oldest and most respected cowboys in the crew. They've shown they can do all the jobs and after years of getting dirty, they get the cleanest, least dangerous job of the day. But putting the iron on means steady hands and using the right pressure, enough to leave a clear mark, but gently enough not to burn through the hide. A brand has to be clean and positioned right, every time.

The cutters are responsible for castrating bull calves. The cow boss will pick a top hand for this job, often the cowboy with

SPRING ROUNDUP AT THE OH RANCH

the best "doctoring" skills and the steadiest hands. Cleanliness, patience and being methodical are critical. Steers are easier to handle, more docile and can be pastured with females.

De-horning can be a difficult job, depending on the method used. Some outfits use "scoops," razor sharp pipes which are used to scoop out the budding horn. Using scoops takes a deft touch, a strong hand and a powerful wrist. Others will use hot de-horners, small pipes heated in the same fire as the branding irons. A selection of scoops and irons are available to accommodate varying horn sizes. Removing horns means cattle are less likely to injure each other, and less likely to skewer a cowboy.

The shooter gives each calf a vaccination shot and sprays horns and scrotums with "debugger," a combination of fly repellent and topical antibiotics, to ensure calves heal properly and quickly. It is also the shooter's job to mark the backs of the calves with a grease stick. This mark lets heelers easily see which calves still haven't been branded.

The OH Ranch, nestled in the foothills of the Rocky Mountains southwest of Calgary, has been branding using these techniques for over 100 years. The OH crew can brand more than 100 calves in an hour and a herd of over 900 in just one day.

Cowboys have a unique respect for tradition, and that can be seen each spring at brandings, and during the parties afterwards. They will swap stories and discuss tack and techniques. They'll ask the veterans to tell stories of the old days. But, tradition is only a guide for the modern cowboy. Show him a better way, and he'll do it. He'll use nylon latigos to secure his saddle instead of leather. He'll use ropes made of modern materials. Brandings have endured for thousands of years, starting with the Romans and continuing today in the Canadian West. They continue not so much for tradition, but because no one has been able to show the cowboy a better way.

■

■

■

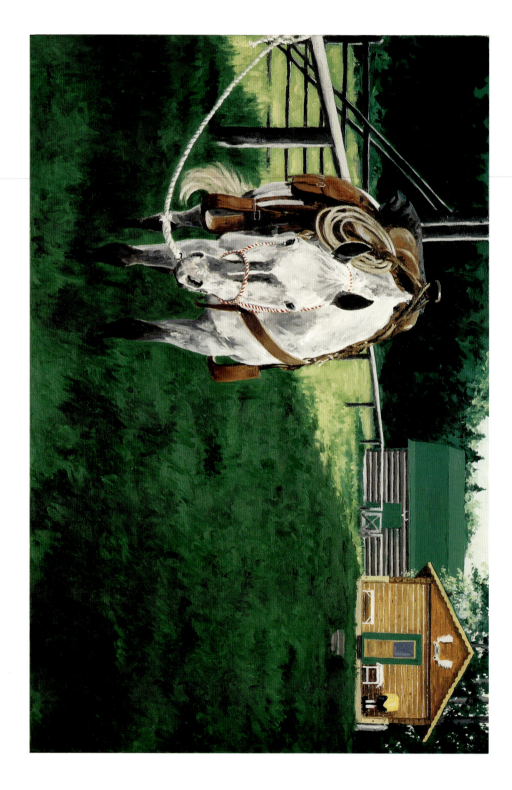

WAITING FOR THE BOSS

CONCEPT AND DESIGN: ROBERT MAGEE

EDITORS: PATRICK STILES AND DENISE WITHNELL

PUBLISHER'S REPRESENTATIVE: SUSAN MUNDL-COWPER

REPRODUCTION TRANSPARENCIES: COMMUNICATION ASSOCIATES

TYPOGRAPHY: LES SPENCER/AD DESIGN

COLOUR SEPARATIONS AND PRINTING: BOOK ART INC.

THE OH RANCH WISHES TO THANK . . .

Patrick Stiles for his special contribution of the essays *Tommy Bews – Making of a Legend* and *Brandings – Picking The Crew*.

Frank and Carrolle-Lynne Duffin and Arthur Andersen & Co. for their assistance in reproducing these paintings:

The Last Crossing – Collection of Frank and Carrolle-Lynne Duffin
In the Land of the Mounted Police – Collection of Arthur Andersen & Co.
The Arrival of the Senator's Rarebreeds – Collection of Arthur Andersen & Co.

The curators and archival staff of The Glenbow Museum, Calgary, Alberta; The RCMP Museum, Regina, Saskatchewan; and The Buffalo Bill Historical Centre, Cody, Wyoming.

Tommy Bews, neighbour and friend, whose expert advice on horses and horsemanship is greatly appreciated by the artist in capturing *Legendary Horsemen* on canvas.